PRAYERS
TO
GROW
ON

PRAYERS TO GROW ON

SUE E. TROUT

LifeRich Publishing is a registered trademark of The Reader's Digest Association, Inc.

LifeRich Publishing books may be ordered through booksellers or by contacting:

LifeRich Publishing
1663 Liberty Drive
Bloomington, IN 47403
www.liferichpublishing.com
1 (888) 238-8637

Publisher's Cataloging-In-Publication Data
(Prepared by The Donohue Group, Inc.)

Names: Trout, Sue E.
Title: Prayers to grow on / Sue E. Trout.
Description: Bloomington, IN : LifeRich Publishing, 2018. | Includes bibliographical references.
Identifiers: ISBN 9781489716804 (softcover) | ISBN 9781489716811 (ebook)
Subjects: LCSH: God (Christianity)--Prayers and devotions. | Christian life--Prayers and devotions.
| Faith--Prayers and devotions. | LCGFT: Prayers.
Classification: LCC BV245 .T76 2018 (print) | LCC BV245 (ebook) | DDC 242.8--dc23

ISBN: 978-1-4897-1680-4 (sc)
ISBN: 978-1-4897-1681-1 (e)

Library of Congress Control Number: 2018904869

Printed in the USA.

LifeRich Publishing rev. date: 06/08/2018

LifeRich
PUBLISHING®

Dedication

This book is dedicated to

my husband, Don Trout
my friend since childhood, Jeanie Clay
and
the Guy Harden Sunday School Class

and in memory of

my parents, Mr. and Mrs. Harold Tate
my deceased husband, Rev. Alex Horvath
and
close friends,
Ethel Morrison and Sister Noreen Hurter, O.S.B

CONTENTS

PREFACE

It all started with my Sunday School class, a class of senior citizens that I was invited to teach a few years ago. We did the usual things – we'd sing a couple of hymns, I'd present the lesson, with plenty of opportunity for discussion, and then I, or someone from the class, would offer a short closing prayer. One day, as I was preparing the lesson, I was inspired to write a closing prayer that highlighted the heart of our lesson, something that they could take home with them and pray through the week, something that might help them understand and remember the inspiration and the truths of that Sunday's lesson. Soon I was writing a closing prayer for each Sunday, and the class members seemed to look forward to each one. Some tell me that they have saved them, and sometimes go through them and pray them over again.

Those prayers were so well received by my class that I dared think that perhaps others might also appreciate them. The prayers were a bit different from the ordinary prayer, as they were focused on some particular idea, a specific Bible story, or a life situation that may be common to all of us. Some dealt with a Biblical theme, some with a theological or doctrinal principle, and others with the life situations that pop up to delight or confound us. And the poetic type of format I used, to make it easier for us to read the prayer aloud in unison, proved to be very popular with the class. It also aids the reader to slow down and think about each individual phrase of the prayer, to use it as a meditation while praying alone.

Some of the prayers included in this book are those which I prepared for my class. Others were written specifically for this book. I have tried to cover the bases, with sections on God the Father, Son, and Holy Spirit, as well as discipleship and life.

I pray that you, the reader, may find these prayers to be inspirational and challenging, and that through them you may grow in your relationship with God. God bless.

ACKNOWLEDGMENTS

I wish to publicly thank my dear husband, Don Trout, for his patience and encouragement as I have spent so many hours in my study preparing this book of prayers for publication.

I also wish to thank Rev. Bruce Jacobs and Nancy Huffman for their help in reviewing the manuscript and offering helpful suggestions.

I send a special thanks to Janice Hughes, who graciously did the illustrations, including the cover.

Thank you to Marisa Martires, Geoff Stewart, Rick VanDeventer, Dana Scott, Rebecca Freeman, and all the people at LifeRich Publishing for their assistance in transforming my manuscript into a book!

And I especially want to give credit to the Holy Spirit, who inspired me to write this book, gave me ideas for the content, and helped me find the right word at the right time. And He nudged me to get busy writing again when life's interruptions slowed me down!

God's blessings on all of you!

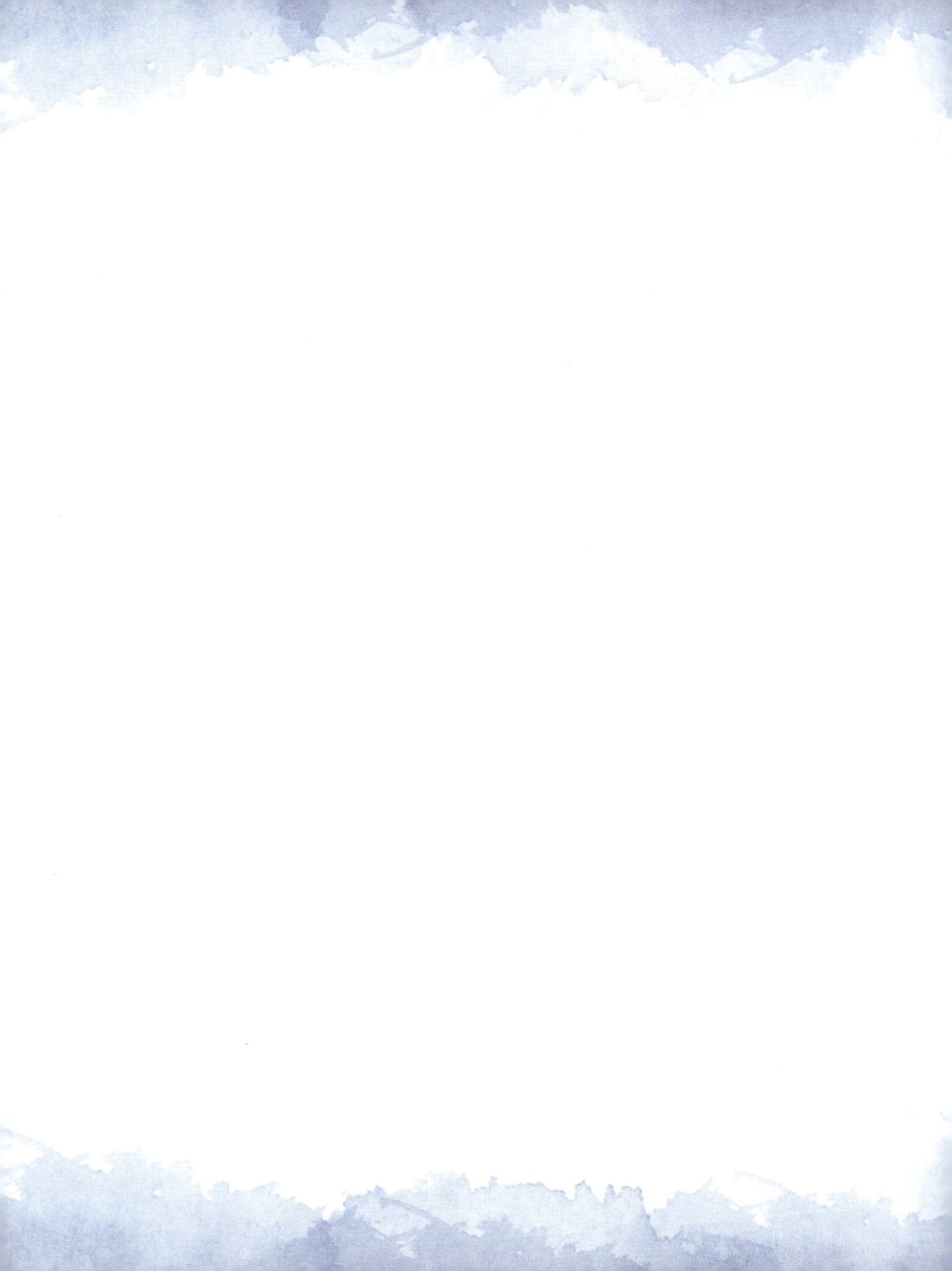

INTRODUCTION

Prayer is universal. It is not limited to Christians or Jews, or any other religion. Even those who claim no religion at all will cry out for help when life or limb is at stake. Even the most self-sufficient will recognize, in very dire straits, that they are incapable of saving themselves. And they will cry out in the hope that someone out there may hear and come to their rescue. Their prayer may not be addressed to God as we know Him, but they have, at last, recognized that they are not sufficient unto themselves. In that recognition, their plea becomes a prayer.

Prayers come in all sizes and shapes, from "Now I lay me down to sleep" to "Our Father, which art in heaven" to the lofty words of the most educated preacher, to the cry of the desperate for help. Toddlers may be taught to pray soon after they learn to string words together into a sentence. The dying may reach out to their God wordlessly. The tears of the grieving may be their prayer, while joyous thanksgiving spills from the lips of others. Some pray only when in desperate need. Some recite memorized prayers without giving any thought to the words. Most of us, if we pray at all, have, at times, prayed in each of the above ways.

We pray for ourselves, our loved ones, the sick, the dying, and for peace, or in thanksgiving. We pray for forgiveness, for wisdom, and for guidance. We pray in church, in a traffic jam, alone, and with others. We pray in silence, in song, in unison, and in our journals. There is no limit to what we can pray for or how we can pray. God hears every one of our prayers.

But our prayers are not all equal. Our prayer for the right answer on the math test we didn't study for is not on the same level as our prayer for guidance in making a big decision. A prayer for a selfish desire is not as virtuous as the prayer, "Thy will be done." Our prayer to win the ballgame is not as worthy as the prayer for the victims of a tornado.

Sometimes we expect an immediate answer to our prayers, and we expect the answer to be "yes." But God answers our prayers at the time that is right from His perspective, and sometimes His answer is "no." Often those things we pray for are not in our best interest, or in the best interest of others. Many times, God has better things in mind for us than we ourselves envision. We don't always understand His answer. But then, neither does a three-year-old always understand why his parents don't give him everything he asks for when he asks for it.

In fact, we often fail to understand God well at all. Even those who sit in church every Sunday do not always understand what the pastor is saying. Even those who read their Bibles every day do not always understand its meaning. Even those who are most learned in religious studies do not have a full understanding. For God's ways are not our ways. His wisdom is in great contrast to our confusion. He is God; we are mere humans. In the words of an old hymn, "we'll understand it better by and by." But we need never expect full understanding in this lifetime. It will be unveiled for us in the next.

That is not a good excuse, however, to fail to pursue understanding while here on this earth. God created us, He loves us as his children, and He wants, more than anything, to have a relationship with each of us. But He doesn't force it. It is up to us to pursue a relationship with Him as He is pursuing one with us. How do we do so? By reading Scripture, by participating in a community with other seekers, and perhaps most of all, by communicating with God in prayer.

The prayers I have written for this book are prayers that I hope can help you in your own faith journey, in your own pursuit for a stronger relationship with God – Father, Son, and Holy Spirit. Some of you are at the beginning of that journey – or even just contemplating whether you want to take that journey. Others may already have a very strong relationship. But none of us has learned all we need to know about God, nor do we have the perfect relationship while we are still on this side of the great divide between heaven and earth. It is my hope that, in some little way, you may hear God's voice speaking to you as you pray the prayers in this book, and that your life may be enriched through that experience.

GOD THE FATHER

God,
    Creator of the universe –
        it is impossible for my mind to fathom
            all that You created.

                From the most minuscule atom
            to the vast Milky Way,
          from the one-cell amoeba
        to the tyrannosaurus rex,
       from the most delicate blossom
      to the mighty sequoia trees,
You envisioned them, said the word, and they came into being!

And the crown jewel of all that You created
    was not the Grand Canyon,
        nor the aurora borealis of the northern night,
          nor the stars that hung in the sky,
            but the human being!
               You made us – humanity – in Your own image,
             and brought us to life by breathing Your life into us!
          You cherished us as Your children.
        Your love knew (and knows) no bounds.

O God, Great Creator –
   O God – *My* creator –
      You created me,
         You have blessed me,
           and most of all, You love me.

                I am a child of God!
                 I did nothing to earn Your favor;
              I am not worthy of Your love –
            but You give it freely!
           I can only join with the universe,
         and rejoice in You.
        Amen.

Creator God,
    You had a plan for all of eternity
        before You ever created anything!
            You knew every molecule that would ever be,
                and when and how it would exist!
                    You had a plan for every star,
                        a plan for every nation,
                            a plan for every human being!

                    And yet,
                        You gave to us — the human beings — free will.
                        We are free to choose to follow Your plan – or not.

                And even more amazing,
                    You are able to work around
                        our obedience or disobedience
                        so that, in the end,
                            Your plan will play out
                                exactly as You intended!

    It is beyond our comprehension, O God.
        But we are only human
            with our very human limitations.
                And You are God.
                    Nothing is impossible for You!
                        Not even dealing with all the mischief
                            that we humans can manage to do!

                        God, it is very reassuring
                            to realize, as we look around at the mess
                            we have made of Your creation,
                        that You are God,
                        and that Your plan for Your creation
                    will eventually be fulfilled.

    You are truly an awesome God!
        None can ever compare with You.
            Some want to think that *they* are gods –
                but how woefully wrong they are!
                    Thank you, God.
                        Amen.

Lord,
　　You have a long history
　　　　of communicating with Your people
　　　　　　through words and actions, signs and symbols,
　　　　　　　and through Spirit-filled presence.
　　　　You have a long history
　　　　　　of saving us from ourselves,
　　　　　　　from our sinfulness and our foolishness.
　　　　You have a long history
　　　　　　of making promises for our protection and guidance,
　　　　　　　and promises of Your loving care forevermore.

　　　　　　　　　And we –
　　　　　　　we have a long history
　　　　　　　　of selective hearing when You speak to us,
　　　　　　　of putting our own wills above Yours,
　　　　　　of twisting and distorting Your plans,
　　　　　and going our own way,
　　　　doing our own thing,
　　as if we were the gods, instead of You.

You are the One
　　who claimed us as Your own
　　　　and gave us the presence of the Spirit
　　　　　to live within us and fill us with Your life.
　　You are the One
　　　who gave us Your Son
　　　　to show us how to live,
　　　　　and to pay the ultimate price
　　　　　　that we might live eternally with You.

　　　　　　Forgive us, Lord.
　　　　　　　Help us to remember that You alone
　　　　　are God.
　　　　Remind us that we are nothing
　　　on our own,
　　that all that we are
　　and all that we have
　are gifts from You –
and You alone.
Amen.

God, Our Father,
   Some of us picture You as an old man
      with a long white beard,
         seated on a throne in heaven,
            keeping tabs on us,
               making a mark in Your book
                  that tells every naughty thing we ever did –
                  kind of a Santa Claus figure,
                     but more fiercely judgmental!

                        But that's not who You are at all!
                     You are a father who delights in his children!
                  You are a peacemaker.
               Far from being vindictive,
            You conceived a plan of salvation
         that allows us to be forgiven,
      that opens the gates of heaven
   to invite us in.

Father,
   our minds are not big enough to picture You as You really are.
      We cannot fathom someone who is all-knowing,
                  all-powerful,
                  and ever present.
         We cannot comprehend that You are the Creator of all things,
                     animate and inanimate!
         We cannot begin to grasp the enormity of Your glory,
                  Your magnificence,
                  Your all-encompassing presence,
               or the depth of Your love
            and relationship with each of us.

How can we relate to Someone
    so far beyond our ability to conceive?
        Many choose to run away
            and attempt to hide from You –
                    but there is no place to hide that You do not see them.
                Others try to ignore You and pretend You don't exist –
                    but You do exist, and You refuse to ignore them.

    We relate to You by acknowledging You,
        by believing in You,
            by talking to You,
            by loving You,
                by serving You,
                    and by putting You first in our lives.

                    For You alone are totally good,
                totally holy,
                and totally awe-inspiring.
            Amen.

Dear God,
   You have given us all that we are and all that we have,
      and we have given You so little in return.
         You are responsible for our joys and our pleasures,
            and we wonder how we can possibly give You joy or pleasure.

      It is very humbling to learn that You actually find pleasure
            not only in our good works and our prayers,
         but even in the common acts of living –
      those things we do, often out of necessity,
  things so simple that we hardly even give them a thought!

      How is it that the God of the universe
         can be aware of even the little details of our lives,
            much less take pleasure in even the most common of those?
         We stand in awe of One who cares so deeply and intimately
  for common folks such as us.

            You have provided for our welfare,
          given us food and drink to sustain us.
           And then You smile when we find joy in consuming
         the rich and tasty morsels on our plates.
        Your heart is warmed when we sit at table
         with family and friends
           and enjoy the fellowship along with the food.
             Yet sometimes we forget even to thank You,
               to remember that You are present also
                 at our table.

  You have given us so much, God.
    May we always be grateful.
      May we share the bounty You have given us
        with those who have little.
      May we find joy in being and doing
        what You created us to be.
        Amen.

Father—
    Jesus called You "Father,"
        and sometimes He even called You "Abba," [1]
            a term of endearment for a father,
                which we might call "Daddy," or "Papa."

            We know that Jesus was Your Son.
                We know that You loved Him so very much,
                    and that You entrusted Him with the most important task
                that anyone would ever have to do.
            We know that the love You shared as Father and Son
                was a bond that was very deep
                    and would never be broken.

But we are also children of God! [2]
    May we also call You "Father"?
        May we call You "Papa," or "Daddy"?

            Sometimes it seems presumptuous to think of You
                as Father, or Daddy.
            It sounds as if we're trying to pretend
        we are more than we could ever be.

But Father,
    sometimes I need a father
        when my earthly father is not available.
            Sometimes I crave a father's love.
                Sometimes I need his wisdom and guidance.
                    I often need his forgiveness and reassurance.

    Come to me, Papa, when I am hurting.
        Show me the way, Daddy, when I am lost.
            Hold me tight, Abba, when I am afraid.

            And listen to me, Abba,
                when I need someone to share my joy!
        Rescue me, Papa, when I stray away from You.
    Reassure me, Daddy, when I feel so all alone.

I put my trust in You, Father,
    and thank You for being my loving Papa. Amen.

[1] Mark 14:36   [2] John 1:12

9

Lord God,
from the moment You created the first human being,
it was Your intention to have a personal relationship
with every one of us.
You lovingly created us.
You created us to be Your children,
Your companions;
You rejoiced in our being.

But we had an independent streak.
We chose to do things our way;
we disobeyed the simple rules You laid down.
We failed to appreciate all the good things You gave us.
Instead, we invented sin.

Our sin separated us from You.
But it didn't cause You to love us less.
You still wanted us to be Your children,
Your companions.
You still wanted to shower us with blessings.

We strayed from You,
but You were not satisfied to let us go.
So You scattered little bread crumbs
to entice us to come back to You.
You whispered to us in our dreams,
saying, "Come to Me,
I am the one who loves you most."

We weren't aware that You were responsible
for the good things that came into our lives.
But those good things prepared us;
they softened our hearts to respond
to Your invitation to come back home
to You.

God, that invitation is not just for humanity as a whole.
it is for every individual.
It is for me.
May I come home to You at last?
Father, I'm ready to come home.
Amen.

Loving Father,
The promise You made to Your people
thousands of years ago when they were captives in Babylon,
is a promise that You still offer us:

"Surely I know the plans I have for you,...
plans for your welfare and not for harm,
to give you a future with hope.
Then, when you call upon Me
and come and pray to Me,
I will hear you.
When you search for Me,
you will find Me;
if you seek Me with all your heart
I will let you find Me...." You said. [1]

Lord, Your promise is so comforting!
It is so hopeful!
Your promise offered hope and purpose
to those taken from their own land
by foreign conquerors;
it offers no less hope
to us today
as we struggle with discouragement,
lack of understanding or purpose,
fears for our futures,
loneliness, depression,
or the consequences of our sins.

Help us—
help me—
to trust in Your promise, Lord.
Hear me when I pray to You.
May I earnestly search for You with all my heart,
knowing that You will let me find You.
For You are my God, my Creator;
You love me,
and You will not let me down.
Amen.

[1] Jeremiah 29:11-14

Almighty God,
  You, and You alone, are holy.
    You are all-knowing,
      all-powerful,
        and ever-present.
          I worship and adore You.

          Angels sing of your glory:
            "Holy, holy, holy, is the Lord of hosts;
              the whole earth is full of His glory." [1]
            Christians around the world join in the chorus:
          "Holy, holy, holy is the Lord our God."

Holiness, though, is not something humanity can truly understand.
  It is so far above us.
    It is goodness stretched to infinity.
      It is love without boundaries.
        It is limitless power used only for ultimate good.

            Your holiness,
              and everything about You
                is without limits.
              But we, Lord, live limited lives
                with limited abilities
              in a limited world.
            Even our imaginations cannot stretch far enough
          to envision the scope of Your holiness.

But we do not need to understand.
  We are not asked to explain.
    We are not expected to be holy like You,
      for You alone are holy.

            All that is asked of us
              is to worship You, our God.
            We cannot be the source of light and love and goodness,
          but we may reflect Your light and love and goodness
        to the world around us.

May we worship You with our whole being,
  and reflect Your holiness to a world that sorely needs it.   Amen.

[1] Isaiah 6:3b

GOD THE SON

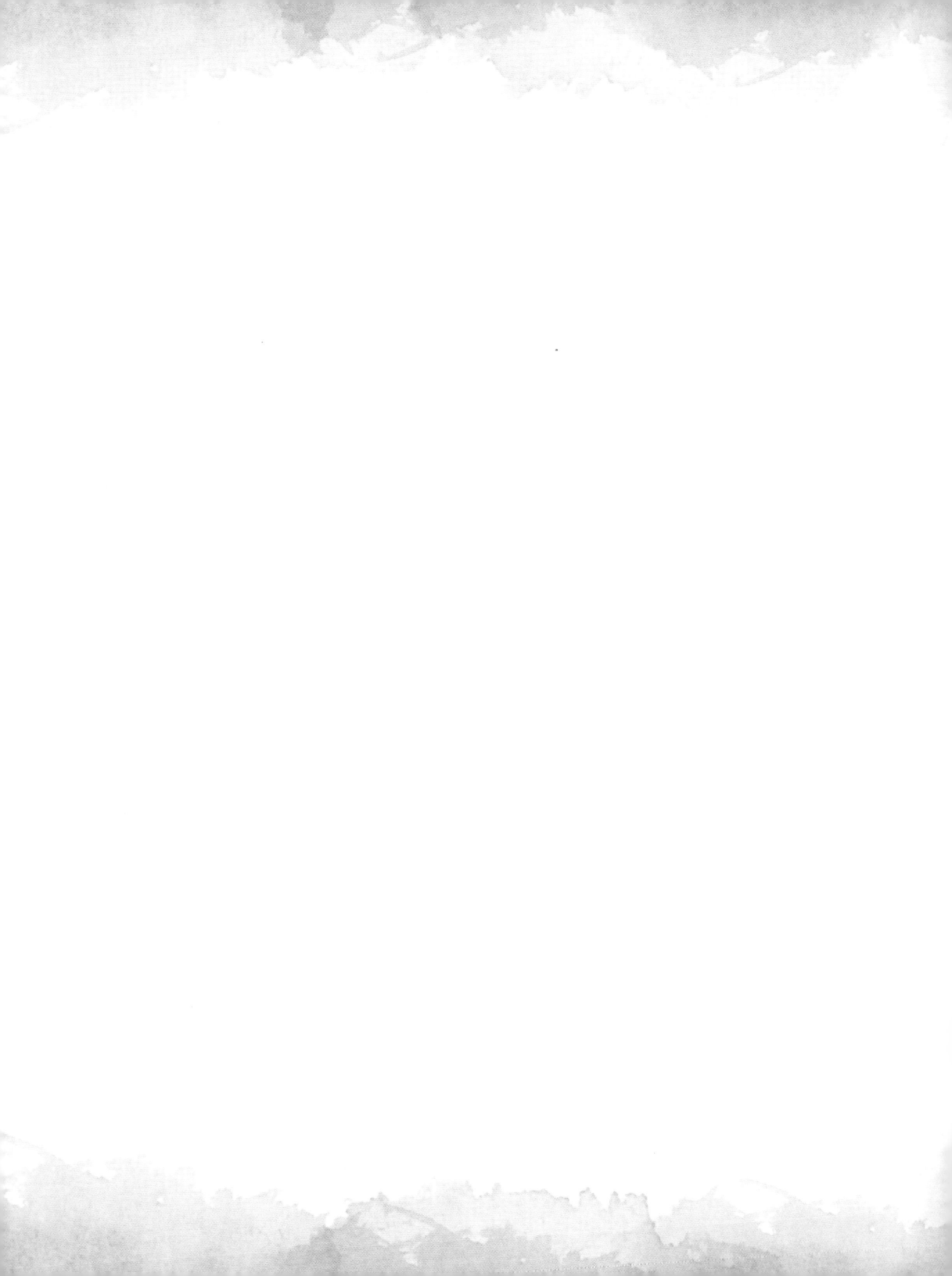

Infant holy, Infant lowly,
     God incarnate, [1] gift of love.
          Tiny baby in a manger,
               come to save us, from above.
                         Son of Mary, yet so holy,
                         Son of God, yet mortal wholly,
                         sent to earth to prove God's love.

Cattle lowing, donkeys braying,
     echo angels' songs of joy.
          Hallelujah, God in heaven
               has sent us this holy boy!
                         He has left his throne in heaven,
                         so that we may be forgiven
                         and our sins may be destroyed.

He will grow to be a leader
     pointing to his Father God.
          He will teach us to be holy,
               help us choose that which is good.
                         He will feed us, He will heal us,
                         He will wipe our tears away.
                         He will show us how to pray.

He was sent to be our Savior,
     to redeem us from our sin.
          The cross loomed high on the horizon,
               'twas so hard to take it in.
                         How He suffered as He hung there,
                         yet forgave them for their sins,
                         opening heaven to let them in.

The grave is empty, Christ is risen,
     a new era has begun.
          Jesus' mission is fulfilled now;
               the crowning glory of the Son.
                         From our sins He came to save us,
                         conquered death forevermore,
                         now the victory is won!

[1] God incarnate: the Son of God took on bodily form, being born of his mother, Mary.
He thus is truly human, yet also remains truly God.

Christ Jesus,
   You came to us
      as a tiny infant,
         just like everyone else at the start,
            totally dependent on others for all Your needs,
          yet sweet and soft and cuddly.

               But You were not just another one of us.
             Few realized that this tiny baby,
           while fully human,
         was also the Son of God.

As human, You were a newborn,
    starting on Your life's journey just like the rest of us did.
       But as Son of God
         (member of the Holy Trinity),
           You had existed from the very beginning! [1]

          Heaven was Your home from the beginning.
        But there was a need on earth
      that no one else could fill.
     Humanity, the jewel of God's creation,
had become tarnished with sin.

From the beginning of humankind,
    we humans have always coveted more.
       Being children of God was not enough –
      we wanted to be in charge,
        to put ourselves first;
          we wanted to be like God.

        So we disobeyed.
        We went our way instead of God's.
       We alienated ourselves from God;
      the tarnish of our sins eroded our whole being,
    and we could not fix it.

Only God – the Father, Son, and Spirit –
could remove the tarnish of our sins,
and prevent it from utterly destroying us.

But it would be costly – very costly.
God couldn't wave a magic wand to remove our sins.

God must join the human race,
live a human life free from sin,
and then relinquish that sinless life,
that its lifeblood would wash away the tarnish –
the sin – and restore our relationship with God.

And You, the Son of God,
were the only One who could carry out the plan.
You became man, but did not sin.
You taught, You healed, You showed people how to live.
And then, You went as a lamb to the slaughter,
a sacrificial lamb,
and gave Your life
to wash away our sin.

Jesus Christ,
Son of God,
we owe You our all.
Amen.

[1] John 1:1 (Here John uses "Word" to refer to Jesus.)

Jesus our Lord,
    You revealed Your identity in the synagogue at Nazareth.
        You read from the book of Isaiah
            and declared that his prophecy
                was fulfilled that very day in You.
                    But the people,
                    Your own townspeople,
                    didn't believe. [1]

The prophecy was fulfilled in an even more significant way
                    a few years later,
                        when You hung on a cross
                            to redeem your people, the sinners –
                and when You left an open grave
                    because death had no hold over You.
            Yet even then,
        so many refused to believe.

The townspeople could not see You as Son of God;
        they identified You only as son of the carpenter.
            Many of Your contemporaries could not see You as Messiah
                because You didn't fit their preconceptions.
                Familiarity, they say, breeds contempt.

Sometimes we Christians may also become too familiar.
            We too often try to make You over in our own image.
            We become possessive of You.
        We hear the parts of Your message we want to hear,
    and discard the rest.

Forgive us, Lord,
        for trying to make You over
            to be what we want You to be.
        Give us the humility
            to allow You to make *us* over
                to be what You want *us* to be.
        Let us hear in Your words
            the message that You intended to convey.
                May we become true disciples of the authentic Messiah.
                    Amen.

[1] Luke 4:16-30

Jesus,
When Your disciples asked You to teach them how to pray,
You taught them the prayer that Christians still pray today:

"Our Father, which art in heaven,
hallowed be Thy name...." [1]

Yes, Jesus, You prayed often to the Father,
and You wanted us to do so too.
You went off alone to pray
when You needed strength,
or answers, or the warmth of Your Father's presence.
You set an example of how to relate to God in prayer.

You prayed for us, Lord:
"I ask...on behalf of those who will believe in Me...
that they may all be one....
so that the world may know that You have sent Me
and have loved them even as You have loved Me." [2]

You prayed that difficult prayer in the Garden:
"Father, if You are willing, remove this cup from Me;
yet, not My will but Yours be done." [3]
And on the cross You prayed,
"Father, forgive them, for they know not what they do." [4]

You prayed often and deeply to Your Father;
yet, Jesus, Your whole life was a prayer.
Everything You did, everything You said,
was an expression of Your love for Your Father,
as well as for those You prayed for,
and for the world.

Jesus, teach me to pray.
Help me to pray the words of the prayer
we call the Lord's Prayer
not just with my lips but with my heart.
Help me to pray with the love You have implanted in me
for those You have given me to love.
May my life be a prayer, Lord,
an answer to Your call. Amen.

[1] Luke 11:2 (King James Version)   [2] John 17:20-24   [3] Luke 22:42
[4] Luke 23:34 (King James Version)

Lord Jesus,
   there were many itinerant rabbis in Your day.
      People were not shocked to see
         You and Your disciples come to their towns.
            Yet, somehow, You seemed different from the rest.

                There was a humility about You;
              You never acted arrogant or proud –
            yet when You spoke,
             it was with full confidence and authority.

You healed the sick, the lame, and the blind.
     Others sometimes healed,
        but Your healings were so full of compassion;
         You never flaunted Your powers
           as if to show off Your own importance.

           Jesus, even the evil spirits recognized You!
         "I know who You are, the Holy One of God!" [1]
       They knew You even when the people lacked understanding!
    And You cast them out of the person they possessed,
freeing that person to be whole once more.

In a day when medical "science" was primitive at best,
     You soon gained popularity with Your healings.
       But You were more concerned with higher things:
    "Strive first for the Kingdom of God and His righteousness,"
      You said, "and all these things will be given to you as well." [2]

         Your message was always about the Kingdom of God,
      even when You didn't call it by name.
      Some thought that You must be the Messiah,
   come to establish an earthly kingdom,
to free them from Roman tyranny.

You *were* the Messiah –
    but not in the way they envisioned.
        You wanted to establish God's kingdom
            in the hearts of the people.
                Rulers come and go,
                    but God's life in our hearts is everlasting.

                            You garnered loyalty and adoration.
                        But You also aroused suspicion and hostility.
                    Your ways were not the ways of others;
                    You didn't fit the preconceived notions
                of how a rabbi should behave –
            much less a Messiah.

    Some might say Your mission was a failure –
        capital punishment is not heralded as a sign of success.
            But those who had been touched by Your message,
                who carried God's kingdom in their hearts,
                    knew better.

                        Capital punishment may be a sign of failure.
                        But resurrection is the pinnacle of success!
                    You, and You alone,
                have defeated Death,
            not only for Yourself,
        but for all who accept Your gift of Life.

    Hallelujah!
        Amen.

¹ Mark 1:24   ² Matthew 6:33

Jesus,
You had a knack for connecting with people.
Old and young,
rich and poor,
healthy and sick,
saints and sinners –
You reached out to all
with compassion and dignity,
and invited them into God's kingdom.

People came to You for healing,
and You healed them.
The possessed approached You,
and You cast out their demons.
Men and women followed You from place to place,
and little children basked in Your attention.

Even those who rejected You
were connected to You.
They were obsessed by You,
couldn't get You out of their minds.
Somehow, deep within,
they recognized who You were
and knew that You threatened
the exalted positions they clung to so fervently.

Some believed You were the long-awaited Messiah;
others thought "maybe."
Some only wanted to be healed,
and then went their own way.
Many paid no attention to You at all –
but others strongly opposed You.

Millenia have come and gone,
but some things seem the same.
Today, many believe in You and follow.
Others doubt; many never give You a thought.
Too many acknowledge You only when they need something,
while others persecute You and your followers.

Yet You still love us all, and call us to You,
ready to forgive and make us whole.
May we all come to recognize and believe in You. Amen.

Almighty God,
   High on a mountain, You exalted Your Son
      in a highly unusual way.
                        Three of His friends were witnesses
                        to a total transformation in His appearance:
                  His face shone like the sun,
                  His clothing changed to dazzling white,
               and long-dead prophets appeared at His side
            engaged in holy conversation.
You testified that this was, indeed, Your own beloved Son. [1]

                  How can we doubt?
                  How can we fail to believe
                  with such overwhelming evidence?
               How can we sit back and observe
               without falling down in awe and adoration
         of Your most holy Son?

"Listen to him," You said.
      Yet it is so much easier to close our ears,
            pretend we do not hear,
               and go our own merry way.
                        For His words
                        challenge us to leave our comfort zones,
                  to follow Your way and not ours,
               to take risks,
               yes, even to "take up our cross and follow...." [2]

God, give us the strength, the love,
      the endurance, and the humility
         to listen to Him –
            to worship –
               and to follow.

We pray in the name of Your own Beloved Son, Jesus Christ.
   Amen.

[1] Matthew 17:1-9   [2] Matthew 16:24

Lord Jesus –
    You knew!
        You didn't walk blindly
            into the trap that was set for You.
                                You knew – and yet still
                        You set Your face toward Jerusalem,
                    and step by step,
                closer and closer, You came
            to the fate awaiting You.

    You didn't balk.
        You didn't turn and run away
            as fast as Your feet would take You
                from the suffering,
                    the rejection,
                        the murder,
                            the grave.
                                The others heard,
                        but didn't comprehend.
                    They followed,
                hungry for Your words,
            but let them roll off their backs like the rain.

    You knew –
        not only the terrible things that would befall You –
            but the Rest of the Story!
                You knew that on the Third Day
                    You would rise again!
                        And that would make it all worthwhile.
                            The others heard,
                        but didn't comprehend.
                    Not until the third day had come and gone.

    We hear,
        but we don't fully comprehend.
            But the Third Day has come and gone.
                And we will follow
                    and meet You one day
                        in Paradise.
                            Amen.

Jesus,
   Are you a king?
      You've never flaunted regal authority –
      yet Your words are full of wisdom.
         You don't live in a palace,
            don't have money or luxuries
               for gifts or bribes –
                  just barely enough to feed Yourself
                     and Your small group of companions.

You seem to be more a teacher,
   or a preacher or even a doctor.
      You have compassion for the people You meet,
         and teach, and heal.
            You have concern for the common people,
               the sick, the blind, the troubled.
                  Such compassion is seldom seen in kings.

            You call Yourself "Son of Man."
               Yet some seem to think you are Son of God!
               Some wonder if you are the promised Messiah!
            Is this true, Jesus?
            Could you be the One we've been waiting for?

The prophet says the king is humble;
   he will come riding on a donkey. [1]
      You seem very humble.
         You are riding on a donkey. [2]
            Are you the One, Jesus?
               Are you the One come to rescue us?
                  The One sent to restore God's people
                     to freedom and greatness?

                     Did you come to save us?
                  Tell us, Jesus.
                  We need to know.
                  Amen.

[1] Zechariah 9:9   [2] Matthew 21:1-11

Dear God,
   You promised a Messiah.
      Who *is* a Messiah?
         What is a Messiah?
            How can we recognize a Messiah?
      You never said when.
         You never said how.
            Scripture references to Him whom You would send
               were shrouded in mystery.
         So how do we know?
            How do we recognize Him when He arrives?
               How do we know that the Messiah has come?

   Those questions plagued your people some two thousand years ago.
                  We tend to think we know the answers.
            But do we?
               What do we expect of a Messiah today?
            Do we recognize Him when we see Him?
         Do we allow Him into our own lives?

   It took the words of the Father
      and the action of the Holy Spirit
         to reveal the identity of the Messiah –
            even to Him who was sent to prepare the way.
                  Can we then recognize Him on our own?

      Those of His own time on earth were prepared by repentance.
         Can we receive Him with less?
            Bring us to repentance, we pray.
               Baptize us with the Holy Spirit.
            Let us hear the voice of the Father.
               And make us true disciples of Messiah
                  now and through eternity.
                  Amen.

Lord Jesus,
    You are the Son of God –
        but You are also Son of Man.
            You are as human as every one of us –
                even though You are also fully God.

                As a human being with the thoughts and emotions
                of any other human,
            it couldn't have been easy to live
    with the knowledge of what awaited You in the days to come.
        Your soul was deeply troubled:
            "Should I pray, 'Father, save Me from this hour?'"
                – But this is the very reason I came!

    You came –
        because of us.
    You came –
        because You loved us.
        You came because we are mired in sin
            and cannot save ourselves.
            You came to save us from ourselves
                and the sin which holds us captive.
            You came –
                    so that You could share the joys of paradise
                        and eternal life
                            with us.

    Words cannot express our gratitude.
        Nor do You ask for mere words.
            "Walk while you have the light," You asked of us. [1]
            ("I am the Light of the World," You said.) [2]

                    Jesus, give us eyes to see Your Light,
                    even in the darkness of our world.
                Guide our feet to walk in the Light.
                May we be Children of the Light forever.
                Amen.

[1] John 12:35   [2] John 8:12

Christ Jesus,
    We remember You
        as You approached the time
            to fulfill the prophecies of old –
                that purpose for which You were sent.

                    It was a difficult time for You,
                        as it is for anyone who must leave
                        the people they love –
                        and the life they love.
                    Yet You accepted,
                    for You understood the purpose of Your life:
                to redeem those of us who could never redeem ourselves.

    Some recognized who You were –
        the disciples,
            the woman with the nard – [1]
                but none *understood* Your purpose in this life.
                One even chose to betray You – [2]
                    he could not begin to fathom
                        the meaning of Your life.

                    You blessed the bread and the cup;
                    You shared it with your closest friends.
                    You told them it was Your body and blood.
                    You told them it was the blood of the covenant,
                    poured out for many.
                    You told them You would not drink the wine again
                until You drank it in the Kingdom of God. [3]

    They did not understand.
        Even two thousand years later,
            we still do not understand.
                Your holiness is more than our minds can take in.
                    Your sacrifice, more than we can absorb.

                    We can only stand in awe and worship You,
                    and try our very best to follow You.
                We love you, Jesus, our Lord and our Redeemer.
                    Amen.

[1] John 12:1-8   [2] Matthew 26:14-16, 47-50   [3] Matthew 26:26-29

Lord Jesus,
    We remember the night
       that You were all alone
          even though surrounded by Your friends.

              It was a night of anguish,
                a night when You were faced with Your fears
            as never before.
            It was a night when the reality of the purpose
          of Your incarnation,
        and the price that would be exacted,
      was more clear than ever before.

Jesus—
    You *knew* that it was possible to avoid the destiny laid out for You.
      You knew that You could walk away free,
        that the Father was able to "remove this cup" from You. [1]
        What a temptation that must have been –
          surely more difficult than the temptation in the wilderness
          three short years before! [2]

            But You no sooner uttered
          "let this cup pass from Me,"
        than You embraced Your role, saying,
       "yet not what I want but what You want." [3]
      You would not walk away and leave us behind, abandoned.

And while you wrestled with these agonizing truths,
    Your friends slept.
      Despite Your pleas for them to watch with You,
        they could not stay awake.
          "The spirit is willing but the flesh is weak," You conceded,
          forgiving them. [4]

            Lord, we too, have willing spirits.
          But our flesh, like those of old,
        is weak – and we let You down.
      Forgive us, Lord.
      Help us to answer Your call.
     Amen.

[1] Luke 22:42   [2] Luke 4:1-13   [3] Luke 22:42   [4] Matthew 26:40-41

Jesus–
Son of God,
Son of Man,
Messiah,
Christ –

humble,
compassionate,
forgiving,
redeeming,
the one man in history
completely without sin –
why must You suffer such indignity?

First, betrayal by one You had chosen as Your own disciple. [1]
Then, arrested, as if You were a common criminal. [2]
An illegal trial, false testimony, and finally,
the question, "Are You the Christ?" [3]

And when You told the truth,
when You answered, "I am,"
You heard the angry charge: "Blasphemy!"
and were condemned to be deserving of death. [4]

Led away from the court,
You heard the crow of a cock,
and looked down to see Your closest friend
sitting in the courtyard,
face contorted,
cursing and swearing,
"I do not know the man." [5]

You did not deserve any of this.
But You bore the indignity,
and worse yet to come,
for our sake.
You are the innocent.
We are the guilty.
Forgive us, Lord.
We owe You our all. Amen.

[1] Matthew 26:47-49   [2] Matthew 26:55   [3] Matthew 26:63
[4] Mark 14:62-64   [5] Mark 14:66-72

Jesus, Our Lord,
    Bloodied and bowed,
        staggering to keep up with the man
           who carried the cross,[1]
              You finally reached the hillside destination
                of Your last journey.

                    Echoes of metal hitting metal
                  mixed with screams of pain and anguish,
              and bounced off the surrounding hills.

A crowd gathered to witness the awful scene.
      Your mother and other women from among Your followers
          watched Your suffering through their tears. [2]
            The proud, self-righteous ones who condemned you
          looked on with relief and satisfaction,
      glad to be rid of the one who challenged them.
            The curious and passers-by stopped to see
          what all the commotion was about.

          Your disciple John was present,
        and You asked him to care for Your widowed mother. [3]
      Where were the other disciples?
        Were they watching, on the edges of the crowd,
            hoping to remain anonymous
                lest someone accuse them also,
                    that they might suffer a similar fate?
              Or had they remained in the upper room,
           afraid to even show up and be recognized?

For You, and those who watched and waited,
        the time crept by at an agonizingly slow pace.
              The sun went dark, as even the heavens
            recognized the gravity of the event. [4]
        And You drew Your last breath.
      It was over.
          Mourners mourned, and walked away.
            Your body was put in a borrowed tomb. [5]
              Only You knew "the rest of the story."
            Let us not forget. Amen.

[1]Mark 15:21   [2] John 19:25   [3]John 19:26-27   [4] Mark 15:33   [5]Mark 15:42-46

"My God, my God,
    why have You forsaken me?" [1]
      The words from Scripture [2]
        escaped from Your parched lips
          as You reached the zenith of Your suffering
            and struggled to take Your last breath.

            "My Son, My Son,
            I could never forsake You.
            I was there with You as You suffered.
            I felt every blow that You took."

"I wept for You.
    All of heaven wept.
      The heavenly light turned to darkness
        as they nailed You to the tree."

          "I love You with a boundless love.
        My heart broke for You.
        Nothing ever, throughout eternity,
        could take away one iota of the love I have for You.
        Never, never, could I forsake You."

"But You, Son – You alone –
    could do what had to be done.
      The Spirit and I were with You
        as You hung from that cross.
      But only You could pay
        the ultimate price for humanity."

          "I have no human body;
        the Spirit, also, has no form.
        Only You could hang from a cross
        and sacrifice Your human life
        for the sins of my people.
        And it makes all the difference!"

"I love You, Son.
    Had I not, from the very beginning,
        loved You with an infinite love,
            I would love You even more infinitely
                for what You have done for my children."

~~~

"But now You are triumphant.
    You have risen from the grave.
    You have defeated Death –
        not just for Yourself –
            You have rung the death knell
                for Death itself!"

                      "I am your Father.
                  You are my Son.
              I could never forsake You!"

[1] Matthew 27:46   [2] Psalm 22:1

Lamb of God—
    You "take away the sin of the world,
        have mercy on us...
            give us peace." [1]

                    Many Christians recite these words
                in their worship liturgies.
                But what do they mean?
                Who *is* the Lamb of God?
                How can a lamb have mercy
            or give peace?

You, of course, are the Lamb of God, Jesus.
    You *do* have mercy on us.
        You *do* give us Your peace.

                    But why, people wonder,
                are You called a lamb?
                The answer goes back a long, long way.

God instructed Moses to tell the Hebrew slaves of Egypt
        to take an unblemished lamb,
            slaughter it, and put its blood on their doorposts
                to identify those who would be led out of Egypt
                    in the marvelous event known as Passover. [2]
                The sacrificed lamb thus saved the people
        from the slavery they had endured for generations.

                    A lamb without defect was also used as a sacrifice [3]
                offered to God on behalf of the nation,
            or as a personal offering
        symbolically substituting for the sins [4]
    and guilt [5] of the people.

Isaiah, prophesying about the Messiah,
        foretold "He was led like a lamb to the slaughter." [6]
            And John the Baptist proclaimed, "Look, the Lamb of God,
                who takes away the sin of the world!" [7]
                    And the Book of Revelation declared,
                    "for You were slaughtered and by Your blood
                You ransomed for God
            saints from every tribe and language
        and people and nation." [8]

You, Jesus,
took it upon Yourself
to be the sacrificial Lamb
that would take away the sin of the world.

You, like the lamb, were unblemished.
The lamb was without physical blemishes –
but You had no sin!
The lamb was burned on the altar,
but You were nailed to a cross.
The lamb was symbolic of God's forgiveness of sin.
By Your sacrifice, You wiped our sins away!

Only You, Lamb of God,
can take away the sin of the world.
Only You can reach out and offer us mercy.
Grant us peace, O Lord,
grant us peace of mind,
peace of heart,
and peace in the knowledge
of Your saving grace.
Amen.

[1] The "Agnus Dei," or" Lamb of God," used in the liturgies of the Roman Catholic and some Protestant churches   [2] Exodus 12:3-11   [3] Numbers 6:14   [4] Leviticus 5:6   [5] Leviticus 14:21   [6] Isaiah 53:7   [7] John 1:29   [8] Revelation 5:9b

Jesus—
   We rejoice for You!
      You left Your throne in heaven
         to come to earth and bear the burden of our sins
            upon Your own shoulders!
                        You taught us from scripture,
               and by example,
                  how to live a holy life.
                Yet You held us to no exacting standard,
            but forgave our sins,
         and handed over Your own life to pay for them.

   And now Your mission has been accomplished!
      To everyone's dismay,
         Death had no power over You!
            It could not hold You back from life.

            Many claimed that Your resurrection was a fraud;
               one could not die and come back to life, they said.
            Some still make the same assertion.

   But we know that the tomb was empty on that morning so long ago.
      And Your body had not been stolen away by Your friends.
         There was no deceit;
            it was God himself who raised You from the dead.

            We believe.
            We believe because we have known You in our own lives.
            We believe because we have been warmed by Your love.
         We have been comforted by Your presence in troubled times.
      We have known Your forgiveness.

   We rejoice for You;
      We rejoice in You.
         We are so happy to claim You as our Lord and Savior.
            Alleluia!
            Amen.

Christ—
We celebrate Your resurrection—
we celebrate Your rising from the dead—
yet we don't fully understand it.
What does it mean that You rose from the grave?
What does it mean for us?
For the world?

We have been taught that You died for us,
that Your death and resurrection bought for us
eternal life in heaven with You.

And we believe.
We believe that we will see You in heaven,
that You have prepared a place for us there,
that we will be reunited with loved ones,
and sing with the angels,
and be in the presence of God.

But Jesus,
there is more to the resurrection
than just Your coming back to life.
It is more than Your appearance to the disciples
before ascending into heaven.
It is more than Your making a place for me in paradise.
You endured an excruciating death,
and You emerged victorious from the grave
because of Your love for individuals and for the world.

I cannot understand the depth of Your love.
I cannot comprehend Your plan of salvation.
I see a sinful world and think it is doomed.
Yet Your love is for all of creation,
and You have promised to make all things new.
You created.
And You redeemed.
And You will be victorious
through eternity.

Amen.
Alleluia!

GOD THE HOLY SPIRIT

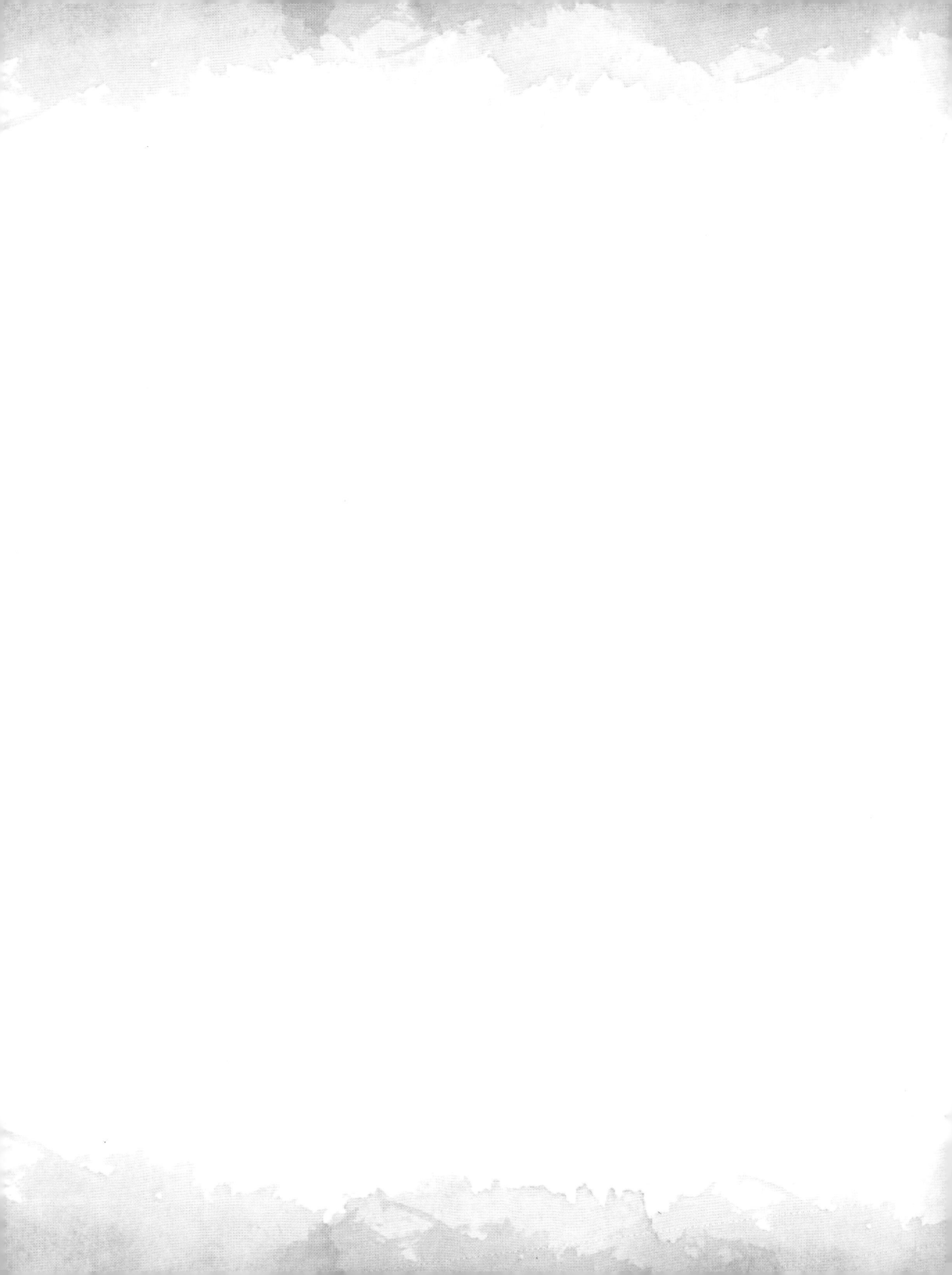

Holy Spirit,
on the day of Pentecost,
You came to Peter and the disciples
and to other believers.
And they saw strange things –
tongues of flames over the heads of those around them,
and in mirrored reflections, over their own!

And they heard strange things –
sounds of great winds
that did not blow things away,
sounds of their own tongues and those of others,
speaking in languages they did not understand –
yet recognized by others as their own! [1]

And in that moment of joy and confusion,
You changed the world!
Jesus no longer walked among them in His human body –
but He was with them – with*in* them –
in the Spirit!

And not just with those followers
gathered together in the upper room.
Thousands of others soon knew His presence
as they believed and You filled their beings
and transformed their own spirits!

We no longer see the flames;
we no longer hear the wind,
or the sounds of our own voices
speaking foreign tongues.

But Jesus is still present with us – in us –
because the Father sent You on Pentecost.

Help us to know Your presence, Holy Spirit.
Show us the way to live;
comfort us in our trials;
assure us that we are never alone,
for You are always with us.
Amen.

[1] Acts 2: 1-13

Holy Spirit,
   You gave to the Pentecost believers
      a heart for sharing and generosity.

               These people may not have been wealthy,
               but they viewed the possessions they owned
               as gifts to be shared with others.

   Not only their physical possessions were shared,
      but their spiritual gifts as well.
         They tapped into Your own richness
            and used their God-given talents
               for the good of their community.

   We too may not be wealthy
      as many would define wealth.
         But we have been blessed
            with gifts of the Spirit,
               tailored to fit our own unique personalities.

               Give us a spirit of love and generosity
               to share our gifts with those You lead us to,
               to let God's love pass through us to others.
         In the name of Jesus Christ, we pray.
      Amen.

Spirit of God,
    You have existed from the beginning,
        along with God the Father
            and God the Son.

                You have been called the breath of God,
                a wind from God,
                the Spirit of the Lord.

    The Lord God breathed the spirit of life
        into human nostrils,
            and the first man became a human being.[1]

                You are with us – in us – still,
                God's presence, intimately united with us,
                even when we are unaware.

    You offer guidance, direction,
        to lead us to closer union with God,
            and a much better quality of life.

                You have no boundaries, no limitations.
                You protect us, sustain us, comfort us,
                and fill us with the joy of knowing God.

    You loan us creativity
        that can only come from God,
            that we, too, may know the joy
                of our own creations.

                Your presence is intangible,
                Your influence subtle,
                but You are ever present to us.
                We can ignore You,
                but we cannot lock You out.

Awaken me to Your presence, I pray.
    Let me hear Your whispers in my ear.
        Let me know that I can always call on You
            for wisdom, guidance, and help in time of trouble.
                Thank You for Your presence. Amen.

[1] Genesis 2:7

Divine Spirit,
  You are called by many names:
    Holy Spirit, Holy Ghost,
      Advocate, Comforter,
        Paraclete, Breath of God,
          and many more.

            As God breathed the breath of life
              into the first man, [1]
            You continue to breathe inspiration
          into our lives.

The goodness of our lives,
    the kindness and generosity,
      the yearning for God,
        the loving concerns –
          all come from You.

            Sometimes they come as a surprise!
            We find ourselves doing or saying or thinking
          things we didn't know we were capable of,
        or things that, in our ordinary self-centered ways,
      are not in our normal mode of living.

  Of course not!
    These are the ways of God,
        not natural to mere humans!
          But because of God's love
              and good will for us and those around us,
                He is eager to share His own heart
                  and His own way of thinking
                    with us!

            And You are the carrier!
              The more that we are willing to listen,
                the more that we tune in to You,
              the more we will also become carriers
            of God's love and of You, His Spirit.
          You, Holy Spirit, are inspiration to us,
        and enable us to become inspiration to others.
      Thank you! Amen.

[1] Genesis 2:7

O Holy Spirit,
    I call on You for help.
        I want to be good,
            and honest,
                and faithful.
                    I have good intentions,
                      and yet—
                            how often I fail to live as Christ asks me to.

                            I am the daughter of Eve
                        (or the son of Adam).
                  I hear the voice of the serpent,
              and it is so appealing.
            It promises power,
        or status,
        or sensual pleasures —
      or whatever I think I'm lacking at a given moment.
    The serpent lies.
        But I feel compelled to check it out;
           surely my life would be better
              if I had whatever it is he offers. [1]

The apostle Paul lamented,
    "For I do not do the good I want,
        but the evil I do not want is what I do." [2]
        I guess that puts me in good company,
            but like Paul,
                I want to discard that weakness,
                    and be the person Christ calls me to be.

                        I need your help, O Spirit.
                    Give me the strength to say no
                to any temptation the serpent
            (or Satan) offers me.
        Help me to keep my focus on Christ,
      and not on my own desires.
    Help me to respond to the needs of others
  and not center my attention on myself.
    Give me the grace to seek God's will
        and the strength of spirit to follow it joyfully. Amen.

[1] Genesis 3:1-7   [2] Romans 7:19

GOD THE TRINITY

Father, Son, and Holy Spirit,
from the beginning
You have existed.
You have been intertwined,
three Ones who together make one God.

Our tiny minds, God,
are unable to grasp the full reality
of Your trinitarian oneness.
You are three separate persons,
but together you are one God.

The Father is God;
Jesus is God;
the Holy Spirit is God.
But the Father is not Jesus,
and He is not the Holy Spirit.
Jesus is not the Father,
and He is not the Holy Spirit.
The Holy Spirit is not the Father,
and He is not the Son.

You are not in competition,
nor are You in conflict.
You work together
to bring harmony to all creation.
Your roles are separate,
yet overlapping.

I may call each of You God.
But I relate to You differently.
I relate to You, Father, as Your child,
and know You as my Supreme Authority.
I relate to You, Jesus, as redeemed to Redeemer,
and see You as teacher, healer, friend, and example.
I relate to You, Holy Spirit,
as the One who dwells within me,
as my guide, my inspiration, my advocate.

And I worship You, the Three and the One.
I pray to you individually and as one God.
I love You, and I owe You my all.
Blessed are You, God – Father, Son, and Holy Spirit. Amen.

O God,
  our Trinitarian God,
    the reality of "Trinity" is so difficult
      for many Christians to understand.

          We know in our minds that You are
          "God in three persons,"
          but such a concept is difficult to grasp.

So often,
  though we *acknowledge* Father, Son, and Holy Spirit,
    individuals *identify* primarily with one of the three.

          Upon hearing the name "God,"
          the minds of many Christians
          immediately jump to the Father.
        The Son and the Holy Spirit
          may be recognized, but not addressed,
      as "God."

Some relate primarily to the Father.
  They direct their prayers to the Father.
    They remember Jesus for his earthly life;
      but they may find it difficult
        to envision the resurrected, eternal Son.
        The Spirit seems ethereal –
          how does one relate to a "Ghost"?

          Other Christians relate primarily to the Son.
          Jesus was human, just like us.
          The Bible tells us stories of Jesus
        that we can relate to.
      The Father may seem more remote,
  and the Spirit cannot be envisioned.

And some Christians relate most strongly
    to the Holy Spirit,
      for they have a strong awareness
        of His presence in their lives,
          a conduit, so to speak,
            connecting them to Father and Son.

You, God,
are Father, Son, *and* Holy Spirit.
You are happy to hear our prayers,
regardless of how we address them.
You are happy whenever we reach out
for a relationship with You,
regardless of whether that relationship
seems closest with Father, Son, or Spirit.

But You have more to offer us
if we build a strong relationship
with the Father
and the Son
and the Spirit!

Like in any family,
Father, Son, and Spirit
offer different aspects
of relationship,
different gifts,
different feelings.

As in any family,
those relationships, gifts, and feelings overlap.
In a family, all (ideally) offer love,
but a father's love is expressed differently
than a mother's, a child's, or a sibling's.
All offer different gifts to the family dynamic.
Our relationship with each family member
is similar, but distinct.
Such is our relationship
with the members of the Trinity.

O God,
our Trinitarian God,
please strengthen my relationship
with Father, Son *and* Holy Spirit,
that I may know and love each,
uniquely and specially,
and be so richly blessed!
Amen.

Holy Trinity,
    the Bible tells us,
        "God is love,
            and those who abide in love
                abide in God, and God abides in them." [1]

                  Your love begins, God,
                with the three Persons,
              Father, Son, and Holy Spirit,
            who make up the Trinity.
          From the beginning, You were Trinity.
          From the beginning, You loved and supported one another.

Love is the essence of God, of the Trinity.
    And love begets love.
        Because of the joy that You found in one another,
            You wanted to share Your godly love with others.

            And so it was that You created.
          You created the universe and all that is in it.
        And You crowned that creation
      with a being You created in Your own image:
"Then God said, 'Let Us make human beings in Our image, to be like Us." [2]

And You loved us.
    Even when we sinned, You still loved us.
        You loved us so much that Jesus came down from heaven
            to be one of us, to take on the burden of our sin.
        He paid the price that we could not pay,
      so that we might be reconciled with our Creator.

           And then the Father sent the Holy Spirit
              to bring the love of God to us in a more personal way.
          The Spirit of God himself has come to dwell within us,
        making us carriers of God,
      allowing God's love to flow through us to others –
if we are only open to His presence and action in us.

Holy Trinity,
    how marvelous You are! Amen.

[1] I John 4:16b   [2] Genesis 1:26a (New Living Translation)

DISCIPLESHIP

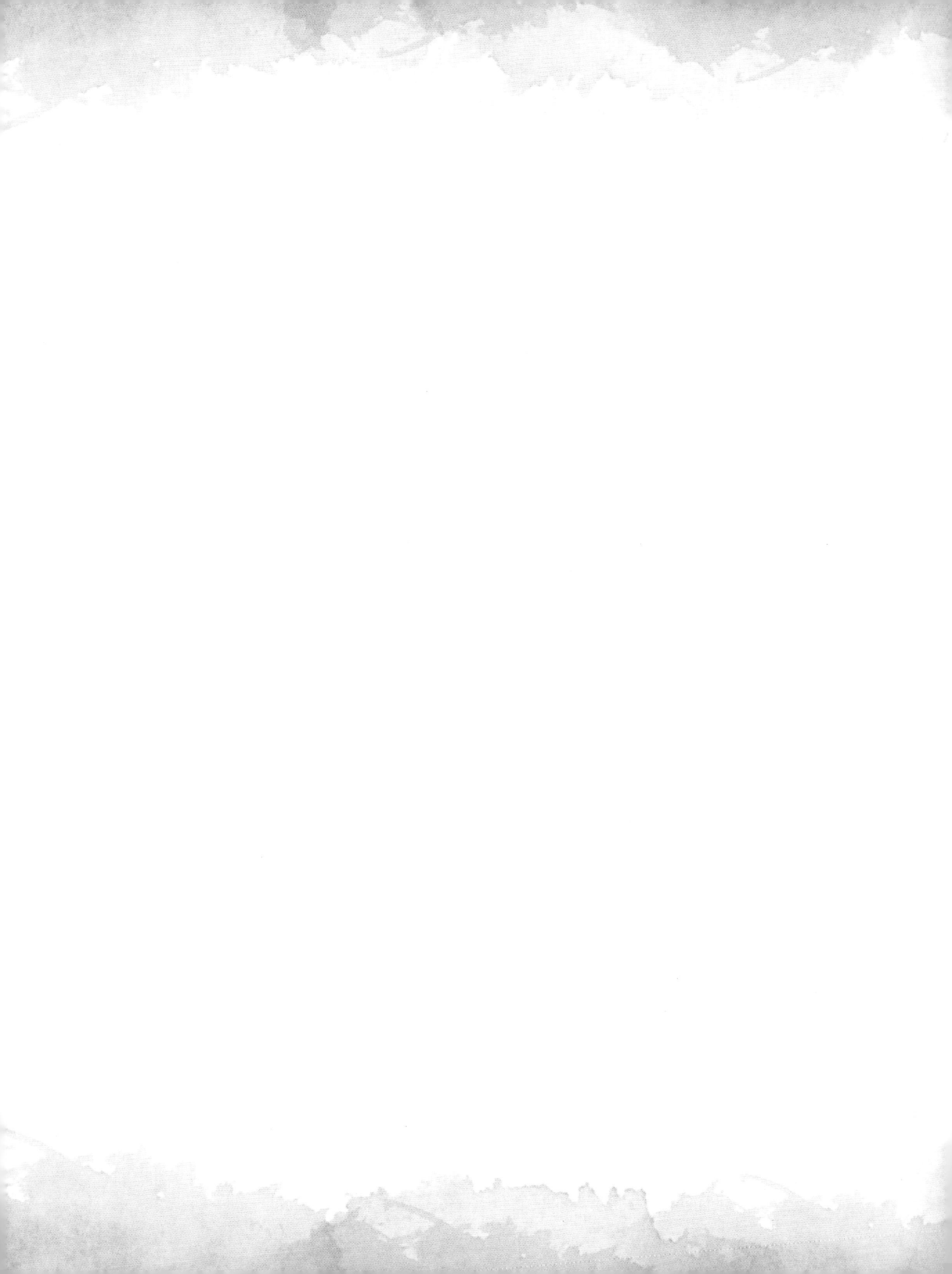

Jesus,
Long ago, You called twelve to be Your disciples,
Your closest companions,
Your friends and assistants.

But many others also followed You;
they walked with You and the twelve
whenever You came through their neighborhoods;
they gave You food and drink;
they asked You questions;
they asked for – and received –
healings and exorcisms and advice.
These also were disciples.

You no longer walk through the countryside with the twelve,
nor speak to gatherings on a mountainside or a seashore.
But You still need disciples –
people who listen to Your words,
people who turn to You for advice,
(or healing, or exorcism)
people who love You
and want to serve You,
and to follow in Your ways.

Jesus, You are our Lord and Savior!
We want to be Your disciples.
We want to follow You,
to love You,
to obey You.
Help us to be true to You always!
Amen.

Lord Jesus,
　　Shortly before Your ascension into heaven,
　　　　You gave Your disciples an assignment –
　　　　　　a big assignment,
　　　　　　　　a mind-boggling assignment.
　　　　　　　　　　"You will receive power
　　　　　　　　　　　when the Holy Spirit comes upon you," You said.
　　　　　　　　"And you will be my witnesses,
　　　　　　　　　　in Jerusalem,
　　　　　　　　　　　　in all Judea, in Samaria,
　　　　　　　　　　　　　　and to the ends of the earth." [1]

You spoke to Your disciples,
　　but was the assignment only for them?
　　　　Was it only for other leaders of the church
　　　　　　who would take their place when they were gone?
　　　　　　　　　Or did the assignment extend
　　　　　　　　　to ordinary Christians too?
　　　　　　　　To those who did not walk with You on earth,
　　　　　　　those who are not theologians or pastors,
　　　　　　those whose ordinary jobs and responsibilities
　　　　tie them down ?

Christ Jesus, what does it mean to witness?
　　Are You calling me to tell others about You?
　　　　Are You calling me to live in such a way
　　　　　　　　that others can see You in my life?
　　　　　　If I am not an authority on Scripture,
　　　　　　　　can I still give witness to You?

Lead me, Lord, with the help of the Holy Spirit,
　　to accept my assignment
　　　　to tell others, and to show others just who You are.
　　　　　　Amen.

---

[1] Acts 1:8

Jesus,
what does discipleship really mean?
Does it mean that we get to "hang around" with You all day,
listening to Your words and witnessing Your miracles?
Does it mean that we are to serve on church committees,
work on money making projects,
sing in choir or paint the church kitchen?
Does it mean that we understand everything we read in the Bible,
or hear in a sermon?
Will we get special honors in heaven or on earth
for positions we have held –
or nice things we have done?

What do You ask of us, Jesus,
as 21st century disciples?
We cannot follow You around on foot,
going from one place to another,
finding a place for You to sleep and eat,
engaging in crowd control,
or even trying to protect You
from those who would harm You!

Take last place and be the servant of everyone else? [1]
Welcome little children on Your behalf? [2]
Drink from the bitter cup of suffering You are about to drink? [3]
Turn from our selfish ways, take up our crosses, and follow You? [4]

This isn't what we had in mind, Lord!
We expected perks as disciples!
We wanted to be close to You,
to be encouraged and consoled,
to feel good about You, and about ourselves,
and our place in the world!

But You asked us to follow You,
and the path that You took led to a cross!
Help us to turn from our selfish ways,
and take up whatever crosses may be ours,
and follow You wherever You lead us –
for You are our Lord –
and we are Your disciples. Amen.

[1] Matthew 20:26-28   [2] Matthew 19:14   [3] Matthew 20:22   [4] Matthew 10:38

Jesus,
    We tend to think of ourselves as individuals,
        independent, responsible for our own actions and decisions,
        accountable only for those things
            that we choose to do or not to do.

                But You say that You are the vine
            and we are Your branches.
            You tell us that we must bear fruit –
         but that we can do so only by remaining in You! [1]

    We tend to think of You as someone separate from us,
        someone far above us.
            You, after all, are God,
                and we are mere mortals,
                    unworthy to claim to be a part of You!

                But You tell us that as Your branches,
            we *are* part of You and must remain in You!
            You say that if we don't remain in You,
          we will be cut off from You –
        we will bear no fruit and will be destroyed!

    You are saying that the fruit we bear
        comes not from ourselves,
            from our own efforts –
                but from You!

Lord,
    prune us and make us fruitful!
        Strengthen our connection with You,
            that we may be bountiful members of Your body!
                Make us always conscious that only by remaining in You
                    can we be what You created us to be.

    Help us to thus bring glory to God! Amen.

[1] John 15:1-8

O Jesus,
We say that You are Son of God.
We say that You are holy.
We say that You are the awaited Messiah, the Christ.

We read that You turned to Your Father when troubled,
that You spent much time alone in prayer.
We read that You turned Satan away
when he tried to tempt You.

We believe that You were born to do God's will in this world,
that You did it for our sakes,
did for us what we could never do for ourselves.

But Jesus, *we* have such good ideas!
The world would be so much better
if You would just do this or that!
Our own lives would be more productive,
or more enjoyable,
or even more godly,
if You would only listen
and take our advice!

We bow our heads
and speak to You in prayer:
Jesus, do this for us;
Jesus, this is what You need to do.

Jesus,
forgive our arrogance,
our belief that we have the answers
and are entitled to advise even our own God!

Give us the gift of humility, we pray.
Let us remember that we are Your people,
Your disciples —
but You are our God!
Amen.

Christ Jesus,
    Since Your death and resurrection
        and ascension into heaven,
            You have no hands but our hands
                to carry out the will of God.

                Yes, the Holy Spirit serves as Your messenger
            to communicate God's will to us.
            But only human beings —beings with a body —
    can physically do the jobs
that You need to have done.

The night before You died on the cross,
    You told Your disciples,
        "the one who believes in Me
            will also do the works that I do,
                and, in fact, will do greater works than these,
                because I am going to the Father." [1]

                Jesus, we cannot even imagine
            that we could do greater works than You!
        How could that possibly be?

"I will do whatever you ask in My name," You said,
    "so that the Father may be glorified in the Son." [2]

                    "I am the vine, you are the branches.
                Those who abide in Me and I in them
              bear much fruit, because apart from Me
            you can do nothing.... [3]
           You did not choose Me but I chose you.
           And I appointed you
              to go and bear fruit, fruit that will last,
                so that the Father will give you
                  whatever you ask Him in My name". [4]

Christ Jesus,
    take my hands, my feet, and my whole being,
        to do whatever You need me to do,
            to help bring about God's will in the world. Amen.

[1] John 14:12   [2] John 14:13   [3] John 15:5   [4] John 15:16-17

Dear God,
The Church is sometimes called the Body of Christ,
and it is called to do the work of Christ here on earth.
It is called to let Christ reach out to the world
through its members and its ministry.

That is a difficult calling, Lord.
How does the Church know what Christ would do?
How does it know what Christ would think?
Most difficult of all —
How does it overcome the human weaknesses —
the human prejudices,
the human limitations of its members
and its institutions —
to be able to answer its calling?

Only through the Holy Spirit
can the Church truly be
the Body of Christ.
Only by listening, and by obeying the Spirit
can it fulfill its calling.

God, we can do little individually.
Together, with the Spirit working through us,
we can do Your will.

Bless us, O Lord,
with ears to hear the Spirit,
and strength to obey,
that your Church may indeed
be the Body of Christ in this world.
Amen.

Jesus—
    You have called me to be Your disciple,
        and I want to say yes.
            I want to make a commitment to You,
                to go where You want me to go in life, Lord,
                    to be what You want me to be.

                But it's scary, Jesus!
                    I really don't think I'm good enough!
                    I don't want to make a promise to You
                    and then let You down!
                    I don't even understand
                    so many of Your words and concepts.
                    I fear that I lack the strength
                    to carry out what You might ask me to do!

    Then I look at the twelve disciples
        who followed You in Galilee and in Judea years ago.
            And I realize that none of them were perfect either!
                    They sometimes dragged their feet,
                        or gave You bad advice.
                    So very often, they misunderstood You.

                    Yet You loved every one of them
                        (yes, even Judas — though I don't understand).
                    You patiently taught them –
                    sometimes over and over again.
                    And You forgave them over and over again also!
                        And finally You trusted them to spread the good news,
                        the news of the Kingdom of God,
                    and Your death and resurrection,
            and the salvation that You have purchased for sinners.

    Yet You did not cast them out on their own
        to fulfill the assignment You gave them.
            You sent the Holy Spirit to them on Pentecost,
                to give them courage where they had had fear.
                    The Spirit filled their mouths with news of God's love.
                    And the disciples became new people,
            equipped and ready to do the job You had assigned them.

    Take me, Lord, and use me as You will. Amen.

Jesus,
    I have heard You call my name,
        inviting me to be Your disciple.
           Yes! I want to answer Your call!
         I know that You love me, Jesus,
           as You loved the disciples of old.
            I trust that You send the Holy Spirit,
              to guide and direct me and give me strength.

             I love You, Jesus.
           I want to serve You.
           I want to serve the Kingdom of God.
        I want to be a healing presence in our hurting world.
        I want to spread the good news,
      and pass on Your love to those
    who are unaware that You love them.
I want to use the gifts You have given me
to glorify You, and the Father, and the Holy Spirit.

Jesus,
    I commit myself to be Your disciple.
        I cannot promise never to mess things up.
           I cannot promise to always understand
            what You want of me.
              But I will seek Your will for me
                and follow it the best I can.

                And when I stray,
                  as all we humans seem to do,
             I ask You, as my Shepherd,
           to search for me
        and bring me back home.
        Give me strength.
      Give me love.
    And forgive me when I fail You in any way.
    I will do my best to be Your faithful disciple
  now and forever.
Amen.

LIFE

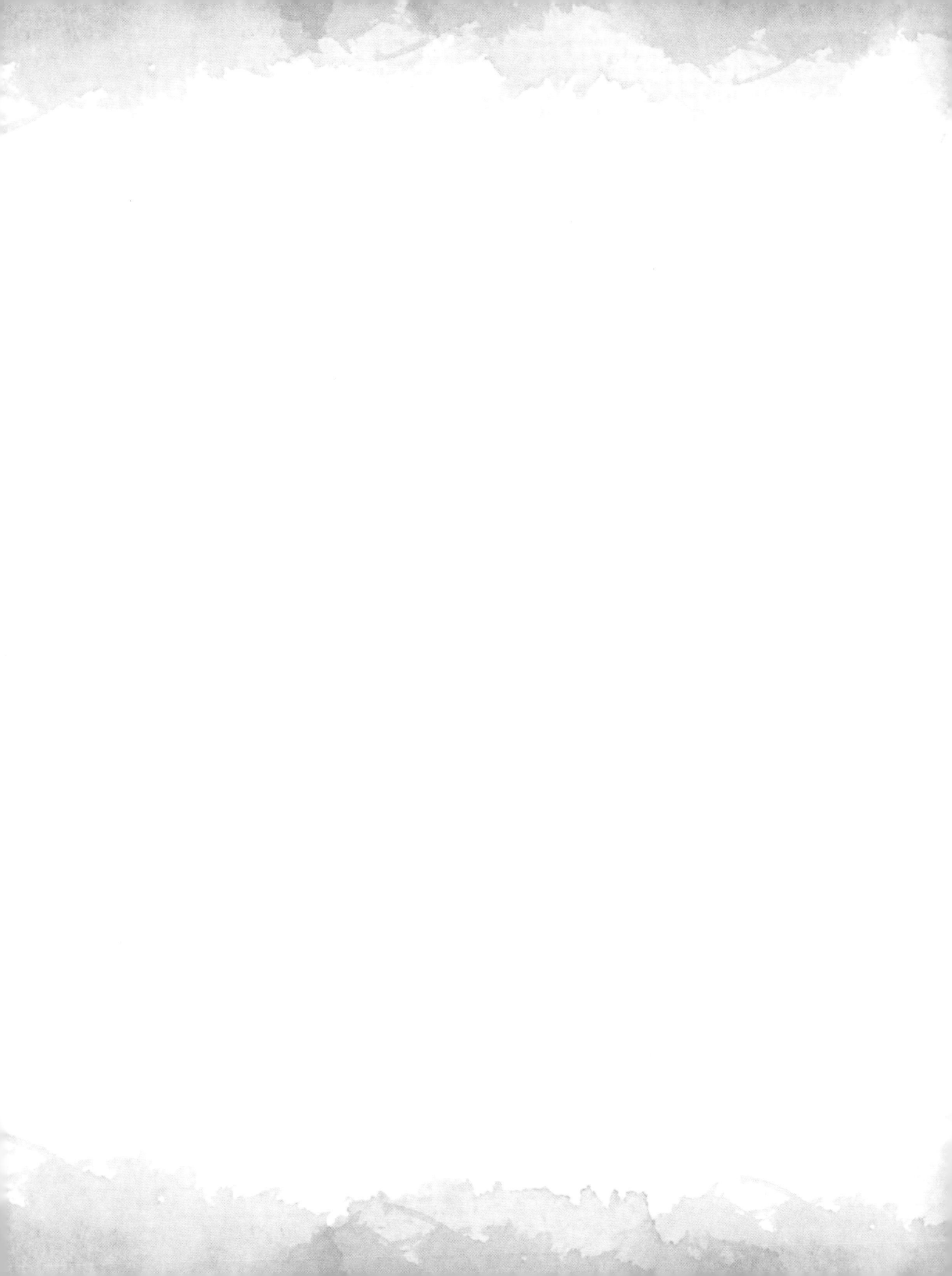

God,
  You are the Creator of all life.
    What, exactly, *is* life?
      What is *human* life?

              A baby is born
              soft and cuddly,
              helpless in so many ways.
              We rejoice and give thanks for the new life.

  A child laughs and plays,
      cries and lashes out in anger,
        dreams of joys and of monsters,
          loves and fears and sometimes hates.

              A teenager dreams of the future,
              tries to establish independence,
              falls in love (often over and over again),
              but underneath, still feels insecure.

  A young man or woman ventures out into the world.
      New relationships, new responsibilities, new opportunities
        fill the mind and the time.
          Growth and failures combine to define a sense of self.

              Midlife may bring stability and confidence –
              but to some, boredom and discontent.
              Relationships and responsibilities may change,
              but life just keeps rolling along.

  Senior years are supposed to be golden –
      but for some, pain or dependence tarnish the gold.
        A time for remembrance,
          a time to mellow.

God,
  life is full of happiness, sadness, joy, and misery.
    You gave us a purpose –
      to love You and love and serve Your kingdom.
        That is the secret of life.
          Amen.

Dear God,
   We sometimes think
      that if we believe in You —
                  if we have faith,
            and try to live good lives,
            and recognize You as our Supreme Being —
         then all will go well for us
      and we will never suffer the darkness and depth of the shadows.

   We've lived long enough to know
      that's not really true.
                  We realize that life is full of trials and tribulations
            for the holy and the wicked as well.
         But we want to believe that as believers,
            we have special privileges.

                  Your heart, however, goes out to *all* who are suffering;
         You do not show favoritism.
      We must be willing to accept what You *do* offer us —
         the gift of compassion,
            the gifts of patience, wisdom, and acceptance,
               the gifts of courage and hope and humility.

   We thank you God,
      for being there for us when we need You
                        even when we're too blind to see;
         for giving us a reason for living
                     even when we hurt so much we want to die.

                  Help us to remember
               that the shadows are penetrated by Your light:
            that three days after darkness covered the land
         for three hours, and the light of the sun was gone, [1]
      the Light of the World rose from the grave.
   That same light is there to disperse our own shadows.

   Thank you God. Amen.

[1] Matthew 27: 45

Loving Father,
  You have given us the gift of life,
    and have made us in Your image.
      You are present to us through the Holy Spirit.
          This realization is awe-inspiring, Lord,
        and we bow in humble gratitude
      and thanksgiving.

  We confess that too often we fail to appreciate
      the magnitude of the gifts You have given us,
        and we fail to use them as You intended.
    Instead, we see ourselves, not You,
      as our primary authority,
    and we seek to do those things
      that bring us only transient joy
        rather than following Your ways
          to find eternal bliss.

          And in choosing our ways instead of Yours,
        we find ourselves mired in foolishness,
      while You offer us wisdom.
    And we suffer humiliation
  when we could have enjoyed fulfillment.

  Help us to be present to Your Holy Spirit within us, we pray,
    that we may know the depth of Your love for us,
      and pass that love on to others
        instead of foolishly focusing on our own selfish interests.

  We ask this in the name of Jesus Christ, our Lord and Savior.
    Amen.

Creator God,
    You who live outside of chronological time,
        yet are ever aware of time in our world and our lives,
            please give us an appreciation of the value of our time
                and our need to use it wisely.

    "In the beginning," John tells us —
        "In the beginning was the Word,
            and the Word was with God,
                and the Word was God." [1]
            "For everything there is a season,
                    and a time for every matter under heaven." [2]
                You walked in the Garden of Eden
                        "at the time of the evening breeze." [3]

    Yes, You seem to have a very specific interest in time,
        yet we take it for granted,
            we use it and abuse it with abandon,
                we fail to understand that it is a gift from You.
                We tear off the wrapping paper
                        and toss it in the trash,
                            ooh and aah at the novelty of Your gift,
                then go about our business never giving it another thought —
                    until the dark clouds gather
                        and we realize that time, for us,
                            is not limitless after all —
                                at least, not in this lifetime!

Guide us, oh God,
    to use our time wisely,
        to love and not waste time with hatred or pettiness,
            to serve and not seek to be coddled,
                to be creative and not be couch potatoes,
                    to grow ever closer to You,
                        and to seek to know Your will and follow it.
                        Amen.

[1] John 1:1   [2] Ecclesiastes 3:1   [3] Genesis 3:8

Dear Father,
You created us to live in time —
a time that has a past,
a present,
and a future.
And You created us to live in space —
a space made up of here —
and there.

Sometimes we tend to dwell too much in the past,
and neglect to be present to our lives today.
And sometimes we look forward to (or dread) the future so much
that we fail to savor present moments.
At still other times, we concentrate so much on the present
that we fail to appreciate the contributions of the past
or to anticipate the promises of the future.

Give us balanced lives, we pray,
lives that build upon the past,
that point toward the future,
and live fully in the present —
lives that enjoy the here,
and appreciate the there.

May we be thankful for the good things that life —
and You — have given us,
and may we learn from the not-so-good,
coming to realize that even those things
that we wish hadn't happened
have given us strength and wisdom.

May we go home again —
to become more aware and appreciative
of the people and forces that have molded us —
and then come back to the here and the now
to live the lives You have given us
and to glorify You forever.
Amen.

O God,
You have created beauty in nature —
in birds and butterflies,
in flowers and trees,
in mountains and sunsets —
and in Your human children —
young and old,
black and white,
rich and poor.

Beauty is that which delights the eyes
and makes us feel good
about ourselves, and others.

But real beauty is more than that.
Real beauty is a reflection of *Your* beauty.
It is far deeper than skin-deep,
far lovelier than the eye can register,
far more profound than we can ever perceive.
Real beauty is not just the packaging,
but the essence of the entire content
of a person's soul.

Make us beautiful, Lord.
Let Your love shine through our eyes
as we interact with others.
Let Your confidence in us
give us a healthy, confident presence.
Let Your Holy Spirit dwell within us
and mold us in Your image.

And help us to see the beauty in others,
that we may never judge them
by their physical blemishes,
pigmentation,
or disabilities,
but may see in them
a reflection of You.

In the name of Jesus Christ, we pray.
Amen.

Thank you, God
  for the gift of laughter!

        So often we take life so seriously
          that we become tense and out of sorts.
          We act as if we have the weight of the world on our shoulders,
          a weight that actually, You carry just fine without us!

The gift of a simple laugh can relieve that tension, Lord!
    Who would have thought that a chuckle could work such a miracle?
    Who would have believed that laughter could heal?

            Some see You as being always serious,
              even harsh or judgmental, they may say.
            Could You possibly have a sense of humor?

    Look at the evidence:
        You created the rhinoceros on the one hand —
          and the peacock on the other!
            You created the gangly giraffe —
              and the "laughing" hyena!

            And You created us!
            You created us with joy –
            and expected us to find joy in our own lives.
    Laughter is an expression of joy, not of sorrow.

"For everything there is a season," we are told,
  "A time to weep, and a time to laugh
      a time to mourn, and a time to dance." [1]

            Your humor is never cruel,
              and neither should ours be.
            Laughter should not be at the expense of others,
            nor should it elevate sinful things.
        True humor is an expression of joy,
          a recognition of the ludicrous,
              a release from the burdens we carry,
                and a celebration of life.

Thank you, God, for the blessing of laughter! Amen.

---

[1] Ecclesiastes 3:1,4

Gracious God,
   You have given us life,
      and You want us to live it well.
        You molded us in Your image.
        You created us to love.
          You designed us to learn and gain wisdom.
          You engineered us to be creative.
            You willed for us happiness and joy.

            Lord, teach us.
           Teach us Your ways.
          Give us knowledge — and good judgment.
         Give us humility to accept from others.
        Give us wisdom to understand right from wrong.
        Give us the desire to follow You in all things.

Open our hearts,
    and open our minds,
       that we may become
         the persons You had in mind
    when You knit us together in our mothers' wombs. [1]

           Guide us to make wise decisions,
         to set right priorities,
        to enjoy the virtuous aspects in life,
       and to reject those values that do not come from You.

For You alone are holy.
    You alone are all-wise.
       But we are Your children.
        Let us learn.
         Let us strive.
           Let us walk in Your footsteps.
           Amen.

[1] Psalm 139:13

Lord Jesus,
  When You walked the earth,
    You spoke often about faith.
      You credited it for many healings.
        You praised the faith of many,
          and lamented the lack of faith of others.

            You asked people to have faith in God,
              to have faith and not doubt.
            You asked them to increase their faith.
          It seemed to be of utmost importance to You.

  We often speak of faith
    as if it is simply belief.
      It *is* belief in God.
        But You seemed to believe
          that it is much *more* than simple acceptance
          that God exists.

            We sometimes consider faith
              to be the same as trust.
            It *is* trust.
          But You seemed to believe
        that it is *more* than just trusting God.

    You wanted us to be in relationship with You.
      You wanted us to realize that we, too
        are children of the heavenly Father.
          And Jesus, You still want the same
            for us, two thousand years later.

Give us faith
  in the Father, Son, and Holy Spirit.
    Give us a close, loving relationship with the Trinity.
      May we not only *believe* that God exists—
        may we *know* You as our Savior,
          know that Your Father is also our Father,
            know that the Spirit dwells within us.
          May we *experience* that relationship
        and know the true meaning of faith,
      the very personal gift from God.
    Amen.

Dear God,
  We learned long ago that "God is Love,
    and those who abide in love,
      abide in God,
        and God abides in them." [1]
  You have given us love —
    love for our families,
      love for our friends.
        But You ask us to spread our love
          far beyond those familiar ones.

              You ask us to love our enemies, [2]
            to love our neighbor as ourselves. [3]
          You even tell us that the greatest love
        is to lay down one's life for one's friends! [4]

  Yet sometimes love breaks our hearts, God.
    Sometimes love asks more of us than we can give.
      Sometimes a loved one betrays us.
        Sometimes a love seems to shatter our beings.

  Give us Your love, God,
      and make us loving people.
        Help us to trust, but protect us from betrayal.
          Help us to give selflessly and not be consumed.
        Use us as vessels, that Your love can pass through
      to those whose needs are more than we could fill.

            Do not let us devalue love
          by wasting it on the trivial,
        by placing its label on lesser things –
      things such as lust, or a desire to control.

  Give us an understanding that real love is costly,
      but that the cost is worth whatever we must pay.
        Help us to remember the price that Christ paid
          because He loved us.
            Amen.

[1] I John 4:16   [2] Matthew 5:44   [3] Matthew 19:19   [4] John 15:13

O Holy Spirit,
You whisper to me
in the depths of my heart,
the Father's words of love, encouragement, and forgiveness,
the Son's invitation to walk life's ways with Him.
You tell me the way I should go,
point out the needs that I should meet,
put the right words in my mouth,
and remind me that I belong to God.

But often I don't hear You.
I have other things on my mind and fail to listen.
I'm too busy to give You the time of day.
What a shame!

Jesus called You the Comforter –
but I am not comforted if I fail to hear Your voice.
You send me warning signals when danger threatens.
But if I'm not listening, how can I respond?
You give me directions and guidance.
How can I obey when my ears are closed to Your voice?
Why do I think of prayer as me talking and You listening,
and fail to understand that perhaps I should be the one listening?

My deafness extends to others also.
How often do I fail to hear a cry for help?
A plea for compassion, a word of advice?
How often, when someone just needs
a chance to express themselves,
do I give advice instead of listening?

If I can't take the time to listen –
to my family, my friends, my co-workers –
or to God—
if I talk past the other,
as if I am the only one with wisdom,
the only one with something important to say,
then I am cheating not only them,
but myself as well.

Forgive me my arrogance,
and open my ears, that I may hear.
Amen.

Dear God,
    You made us in Your own image,
        yet gave us free choice to follow You — or not.

    As we look around the world today,
        we see many who have chosen to follow You —
            those who honor You by following Your example,
                by treating others with compassion and respect,
            and by caring for those in need.

        Sadly, we also see many who have chosen to resist You —
      those who seem to think that they themselves
    are the center of the universe,
        and that You are unimportant —
            if indeed You even exist;

                    and those who worship the baubles —
            (the selfish little delights
        that give them fleeting satisfaction,
      but leave their souls empty);

    and those who willfully defy You,
        turn Your teachings upside down,
            and choose to do evil while scorning Your love.

Lord, today we pray
    for those who are hurting,
        especially those hurt by the evil acts of others;
      for those who are undecided whether to follow Your ways—
        or the ways that You have forbidden;
      for those You care about so much —
            the sick, the poor, the oppressed.

  We pray for those who are struggling to know Your will,
        and to follow You in a world that often scorns Your ways.
  We also pray for those who have chosen
        to follow paths that lead away from You,
            paths that are harmful for themselves
                and for those upon whom they may prey.
                  May their hearts be turned toward You.
                      Amen.

Lord–
We live in a world that often seems so dark,
a world so different from the beauty You created –
the world in which You placed our first ancestors
to be Your companions.

Unfathomable violence is taking place
in areas of the world where Your people first walked.
Immorality is rampant and accepted as normal.
People — even those raised in Your churches and synagogues —
deny You, or live their lives as though You had no relevance.

We have dark places in our own lives, too:
worries about health, finances, and relationships,
concerns about the directions our lives are going,
and our lack of control over things that affect us deeply.

We need light, Lord.
Light that can give us direction.
Light that can give us hope and promise.
Light that can illuminate and help us to understand
the meaning of our lives — and of Yours.

We need light to reveal that the stopping places
in which find ourselves
are not staying places,
but temporary points along the way.
We need light to give us a glimpse of our final destination —
in Paradise with You!

You came among us
to give us that light.
"I am the Light of the World" You promised.
"Whoever follows Me will never walk in darkness
but will have the light of Life." [1]

We thank You and praise You
for illuminating the paths of our lives.
Amen.

[1] John 8:12

O my Father!
Sometimes life seems so hard! So unfair!
I have so many questions.
I feel so helpless,
and sometimes, so hopeless!

Why do babies die?
Why do parents abuse their children?
Why do good workers lose their jobs
and their ability to support their families,
while some real jerks make millions?
Why do bad people go into schools or churches
and shoot and kill and maim innocent people?
Why?

It's hard enough to accept
when reading the newspaper or watching television news.
I don't know those people,
but I still hurt for their suffering.

But sometimes it is people I know
who seem to suffer needlessly.
I may be able to offer a sympathetic word
or help them out in some small way,
but I cannot do anything to change their circumstances.

Sometimes I am the one treated unfairly,
or diagnosed with a terrible disease,
or I lose someone I love dearly.
And I hurt, and no one can take away the pain.
Sometimes it is difficult to remember
that You are always there for me.

But You are.
　　Sometimes I hurt so much that I don't recognize Your presence.
　　Sometimes I even lay the blame on You!
　　You have broad shoulders,
　　　　an understanding heart,
　　　　　　and infinite patience.

　　　　　　You put your arm around me,
　　　　　　and eventually I am able to feel You.
　　　　Healing comes slowly –
　　understanding even slower.
　　But You are with me,
and I will be ok once again.

There seem to be no answers for many of life's agonies.
　　But I trust that You will make things right in the end.
　　Maybe not in our lifetimes.
　　　　Maybe not on this earth.
　　　　　　In our blindness, we cannot see eternity.

　　But eternity has the answers.
　　　　And in eternity,
　　　　　　our hearts will finally find their peace.

　　　　　　May I find my peace in You, O God.
　　　　　May I find my peace in You.
　　　Amen.

Jesus,
Sins can range from an uncharitable thought
to the most heinous crime;
they can be acts of wrongdoing,
or failure to do the good and loving thing.

Some sins are obviously more serious than others –
but all sins should be taken seriously,
for all are an affront against the loving nature of our God.

You often spoke out against the sin of hypocrisy—
a sin that does not often cross the mind as we compile a list of sins.
What is hypocrisy?
Why did it bother You so?

Hypocrisy is the belief – or pretense –
that we are better than others,
more holy than others.
It is the pretension of possessing attributes
that are not truly a part of our character.
And it is nearly always accompanied by
a penchant for judging others to be inferior.
It is a self-indulgent dishonesty.

You denounced the hypocrites of Your day:
"Woe to you," You told them.
"They do not practice what they teach....
they love to have the place of honor....
All who exalt themselves will be humbled,
and all who humble themselves will be exalted." [1]

Jesus, am I a hypocrite?
Probably most people are,
to some extent.
Point out to me my own hypocrisy,
that I may change my sinful ways.
Forgive me when I exalt myself at the expense of others.
Give me the humility that will counteract such false pride.
Fill me with compassion.
Help me to model myself after You.
Amen.

[1] Matthew 23:13, 3, 6, 12

Jesus, our Savior,
   You asked us to repent of our sins,
      and assured us that if we did so sincerely,
         we would be forgiven.

                  Often our pride stands in the way.
               We don't want to admit that we are flawed people –
            and that we are the ones responsible for those flaws!
            Or, we have become too comfortable with our sins
         and have no desire to change.

   But Jesus,
      we cannot imagine the weight You lift from our shoulders
         when we repent and You remove the sin from us!
            Not to mention the joy that awaits us
         when we claim the gift of salvation You have set aside for us!

   So Jesus,
      today I repent for:
         failing to hear the cries for help from those around me;
            putting my own interests above the needs of others;
               neglecting to brighten the days of others
                  with deeds of kindness;
                     presuming that I am qualified to judge others;

                     dwelling on dark and negative thoughts;
                  saying unkind words or doing unkind deeds;
               letting greed, lust, or desire for power
                  lead me down forbidden paths;
               giving in to temptations to do or say or think
                  things that I know are wrong;
            believing and acting as if I am the supreme power in my life;

         failure to recognize and glorify You as Lord of my life;
            failure to seek and follow Your will;
               failure to recognize and praise Your glory;
                  and the following more specific personal sins:.........

Forgive me, Lord.
   Cleanse me of my sin and set me free.
      Amen.

Jesus,
  You were mistreated, cruelly mistreated –
      to the point of death.
    You were the least deserving of such cruelty
        of all the people who ever lived!

  Yet You forgave.
    "Father, forgive them," You said,
      "for they do not know what they are doing." [1]

                    But when people do me wrong –
                  when they cheat me, or threaten,
                or hurt me physically,
                or even just hurt my feelings,
              I find it so hard to forgive.

                  I am so angry, so bitter,
                even so self-righteous!
              I don't want to forgive –
            I want to get even!
          I want them to suffer as I have suffered!

  You said, "Whenever you stand praying, forgive,…
        so that your Father in heaven
            may also forgive you your trespasses." [2]
      Forgiveness means turning my anger over to God,
            letting loose of my desire for revenge.

                It is sometimes so very hard!
              I hold tight the desire to hurt them back.
            But it is myself that I hurt!
          How can I be a loving person
        if I choose to hate, to seek revenge?
      How can I be free, if I am enslaved by my bitterness?

  You didn't say I have to accept them as my best friends.
      You ask me to forgive and let go.
        Help me, Lord.
            Guide me to the place where I can turn it all over to You.
            And then forgive me my sins,
                as I forgive those who sin against me.   Amen.

¹ Luke 23:34   ² Mark 11:25

88

Eternal God,
   Before the earth,
      the mountains,
         and the skies were formed,
   You knew — and loved —
         each one of us.
     You numbered even
           the hairs on our heads
      and the days of our lives
          before the beginning.

             We give You thanks
          for every one of those days —
        even for the most painful —
      for You never left us alone,
     but were always there with us,
    loving us,
   even when we were unaware of Your presence –
and Your love.

From the moment of our conception —
        our beginning —
   we have drawn, day by day,
      ever closer to our end,
         and sometimes that frightens us.

           Yet our ending time in this world
        is not actually our end,
      for there will be a new beginning
     when Your presence will no longer be hidden,
    and we will enter that sphere in which time is no more,
and endings no longer exist.

Help us to prepare for the Life ahead,
    and to live out the remainder of our lives on earth
       in ever-closer union with You.
         Amen.

O Lord,
Death is shrouded in mystery and mystique;
    one day a person is alive,
        laughing and living life joyfully,
            or perhaps ill, in pain, or even unconscious.
        And the next day the body lies motionless and cold;
            an empty vessel,
                devoid of the spirit that defined it.

        We grieve the ones who have gone before.
        We know, in our minds, that death will claim us all.
        Someday, it will be my name in the list of obituaries.
        And I grieve to think that this life, for me, will be no more.

Some quake with fear at the thought of death.
    Life seems so natural; death so unnatural.
        "But I have so many things I still want to do," we think.
            "Lord, just a little more time...."

                We fear the pain and suffering of dying,
                    grieve at leaving loved ones behind.
                Regret the things we must leave undone.
            "Why, Lord? Why me? Why now?"

But we humans can be so short-sighted.
    "It is the end," we think.
        We cannot see beyond the veil,
            the veil that separates life on earth from eternity.

            We do not see You waiting with outstretched arms
                to welcome us to our eternal home.
            We do not know the warmth of Your love,
        preparing a place of pure peace and love for us forever.
            We do not hear the songs of the angels
                witnessing to the glory of God,
                    and inviting us to join their chorus.

                It is OK for us to grieve
                    as we approach the end of the life we know.
                But let us also look ahead to the horizon,
                    for a better day is waiting.
                And You are there, waiting to embrace us
                as we enter Paradise with You. Amen.

My God,
I cry out to You in anguish.
You have given me many to love —
parents, spouse, children, siblings, friends.
But this one,
this special one,
has gone home to You –
and I am left with a void
that crushes my soul.

Love is such a wonderful gift, my God,
and I cherish the memories of my loved one's love.
Not all was perfect – it never is –
but my love glosses over the imperfections,
and my heart aches for the joys we shared,
the companionship, the faith we had in each other, and in You.

My loved one had become a part of me,
a part of the definition of who I am.
Who am I now?
How can I go on when part of me is gone?

Help me, O Lord.
Help me to find myself again.
Help me to regain my balance once more.
Help me to look beyond my grief and sadness
and see that life still offers promises –
and the darkness will someday yield to the dawn.

You are still with me, my God.
Sometimes I cannot see You for the tears.
Sometimes I cannot hear You,
for the silence is all-encompassing.
But I know You are with me.
I know that You love me.
I know that You do not condemn me
for feeling abandoned
even when You are near.

Thank You for the life of my loved one,
and for all the wonderful things we shared.
Thank You for my own life.
Heal me and let me live it fully once again. Amen.

Jesus—
I am a woman — or a man.
I am happy — or sad.
I am healthy— or sick.
I am old – or young.
I am distressed – or content.
I am weary – or rested.
I am busy — or relaxed.
I am *(your name)*.

These are the ways we think of ourselves, Jesus.
But they do not define us.
They do not tell who we really are.

But You said, "I AM."
And Your sayings told us Who You are.
"I AM the Bread of Life." [1]
"I AM the Light of the World." [2]
"I AM the Good Shepherd." [3]
"I AM the True Vine." [4]
"I AM the Way, the Truth, and the Life." [5]
"I AM the Resurrection and the Life." [6]
These words defined who You truly are.

Help us to listen to Your words,
that we might know You better,
that we might better understand who You are,
and why God sent his Son into this world
for our own sakes.

Help me, I pray,
that I may know the true definition of myself:
beloved child of God,
Amen.

[1] John 6:35   [2] John 8:12   [3] John 10:11   [4] John 15:1   [5] John 14:6   [6] John 11:25

Heavenly Father,
     thank you for this life You have given me.
          Thank you for the loved ones You have put in my path.
               Thank you for the blessings of happiness,
                    achievements, and learning.
               Thank you for the opportunities
                    to love and serve others.
               Thank you for the privilege
                    of knowing and serving You.

                    Christ Jesus,
                         thank you for coming to show me the way.
                    Thank you for teaching me how to love.
                    Thank you for healing my body and my soul.
               Thank you for Your comfort and Your challenges.
               Thank you for giving Your life to pay for my sins.
          Thank you for bridging the way to heaven for me.

Holy Spirit,
     Thank you for your guidance.
          Thank you for teaching me right from wrong.
               Thank you for inspiring me to be more
                    than I thought I could be.
               Thank you for pointing me in the right direction.
                    Thank you for being with me when I felt all alone.
                         Thank you
                              for being the presence of God within me.

                         God the Three in One,
                              Thank you for being here from the beginning.
                         Thank you for Your plans for Your creation.
                    Thank you for Your patience and forgiveness.
               Thank you for Your plan of salvation for a wayward people.
          Thank you for being there for me and for all creation.
     Thank you for being my God.
     Amen.

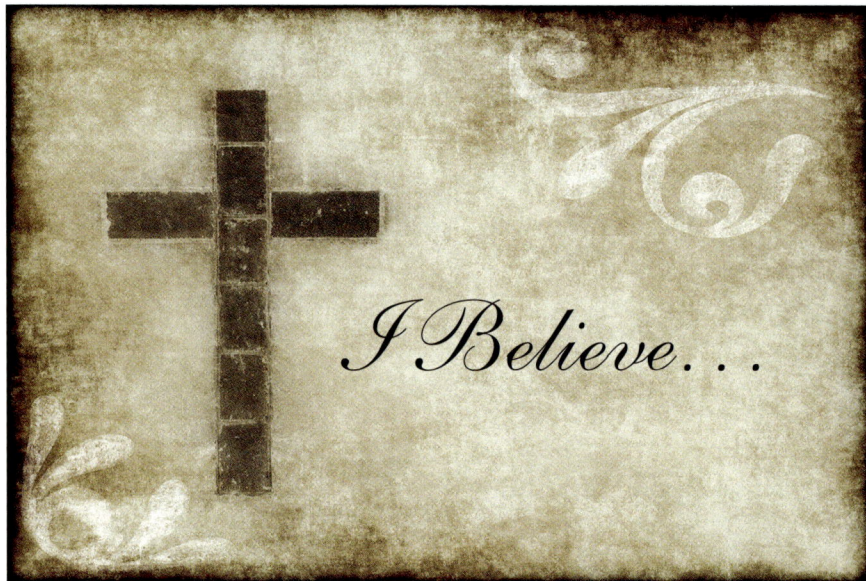

I Believe...

AND JUST ONE MORE
THING...

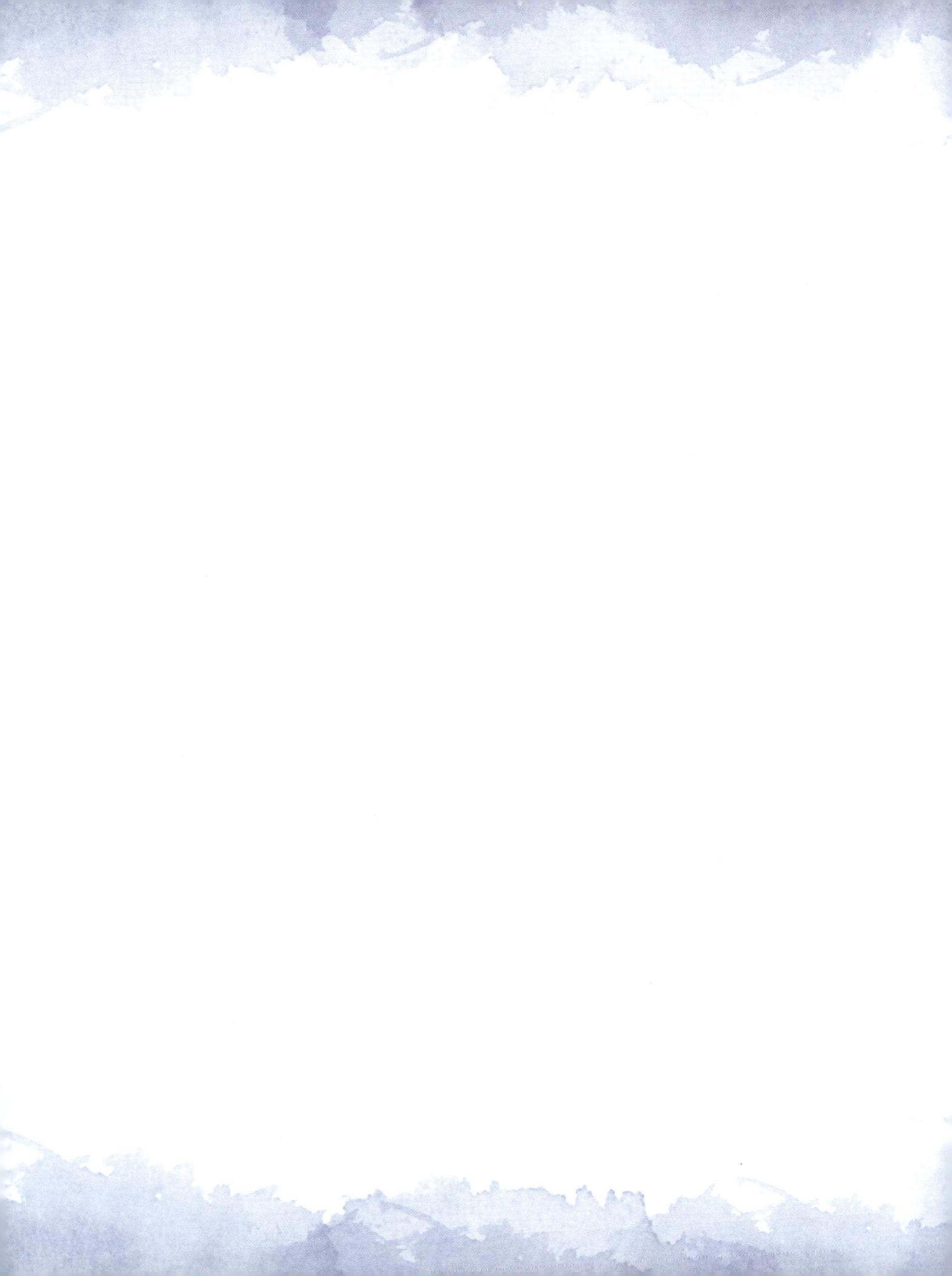

And just one more thing...

The universal Christian church has many doctrines and beliefs that guide it. Various denominations differ somewhat in the details of their beliefs, but most are faithful to the ancient creeds that early Christians wrote to determine and define the basic guidelines of Christian belief. Even denominations that do not accept the creeds in their entirety share many of the basic beliefs cited there. In this book of prayers, I have tried to stimulate the Christian – or the seeker who may not yet have committed to the Christian faith – to prayerfully think about these precepts, which are so basic to Christian belief, yet not always well understood by many believers. It is my hope that the prayers in this book will make those truths more real to the reader/pray-er, and that they will indeed be helpful in stimulating one's growth in faith and in building one's relationship with God—Father, Son, and Holy Spirit.

The two best-known creeds of Christianity are the Nicene Creed and the Apostles' Creed, both of which date back to the early centuries after Christ. Many, but not all, Christian churches recite one of these creeds during worship services, on a regular or irregular basis. Differences in translations and in some cases, denominational tweaking, may result in minor differences in wording from one source to another. I have included the text of these two creeds, as they appear in the United Methodist Hymnal, on the following pages.

But I also think that it is a good idea for the believer to give some thought to his or her own beliefs, and, as an exercise and a way of firming up what one really does believe, to write out their own personal creed. It doesn't need to be fancy or use big words. It might even change a little from time to time as one continues to grow in faith. But it is in one's own words instead of a translation of ancient Latin words and phrases. It reflects one's own values and emotions and point of view. To have that creed, perhaps tucked away in a favorite Bible, is to have something to turn to when faith is challenged, or when one just needs a little reminder or comfort.

I wrote such a creed as a class assignment years ago, and I like to look back at it occasionally as a reminder of what I really do believe. Over the years, I have not found anything I would want to change— but I may see something that perhaps I have not emphasized enough in my own life recently. I may see something that makes me feel especially thankful or brings a smile to my face. I have included my creed also, along with the two ancient creeds of the church mentioned above.

I urge you to write a creed of your own, if you are so inclined, now that you have read, and prayed, the prayers in this book.

THE NICENE CREED

We believe in one God,
    the Father, the Almighty,
    maker of heaven and earth,
    of all that is, seen and unseen.

We believe in one Lord, Jesus Christ,
    the only Son of God,
    eternally begotten of the Father,
    God from God, Light from Light,
    true God from true God,
    begotten, not made,
    of one Being with the Father;
    through him all things were made.
    For us and for our salvation
        he came down from heaven,
        was incarnate of the Holy Spirit and the Virgin Mary
        and became truly human.
        For our sake he was crucified under Pontius Pilate;
        he suffered death and was buried.
        On the third day he rose again
        in accordance with the Scriptures;
        he ascended into heaven,
        and is seated at the right hand of the Father.
        He will come again in glory
        to judge the living and the dead,
        and his kingdom will have no end.

We believe in the Holy Spirit, the Lord, the giver of life
    who proceeds from the Father and the Son,
    who with the Father and the Son
        is worshiped and glorified,
    who has spoken through the prophets.
    We believe in the holy catholic [1] and apostolic church.
    We acknowledge one baptism
        for the forgiveness of sins.
    We look for the resurrection of the dead,
        and the life of the world to come. Amen.

---

[1] The word "catholic" here means universal, and does not refer specifically to the Roman Catholic Church.

THE APOSTLES' CREED,
ECUMENICAL VERSION

I believe in God, the Father Almighty,
    creator of heaven and earth.

I believe in Jesus Christ, his only Son, our Lord,
    who was conceived by the Holy Spirit,
    born of the Virgin Mary,
    suffered under Pontius Pilate,
    was crucified, died, and was buried;
    he descended to the dead. [1]
    On the third day he rose again;
    he ascended into heaven,
    is seated at the right hand of the Father,
    and will come again to judge the living and the dead.

I believe in the Holy Spirit,
    the holy catholic [2] church,
    the communion of saints,
    the forgiveness of sins,
    the resurrection of the body
    and the life everlasting. Amen.

[1] The phrase "he descended to the dead" is not included in all versions   [2] The word "catholic" here means universal, and does not refer specifically to the Roman Catholic Church

MY CREED
by Sue Trout

I believe in God the Father, the creator of the universe and all that is in it. I believe that He always has and forever will love all of His creation to an infinite degree.

I believe in Jesus Christ, Son of God, who was with the Father from the beginning. I believe that He willingly became man, being thus fully God and fully human, in order to redeem humankind from sin and offer them eternal life. I believe that He died on a cross, and after three days He rose from the dead, putting an end to the power of death.

I believe in the Holy Spirit, who together with God the Father and Jesus Christ the Son, comprises the triune God. I believe the Holy Spirit interacts directly with individuals and the church to develop their relationships with and service to both God and other people.

I believe in the church as community of believers who come together to worship and serve God, strengthen believers, and witness to and care for the people of the world.

I believe that God created humans in His image, and loves them so much that he paid the ultimate price to overcome sin and death in order to reunite them to himself eternally.

Amen.

MY OWN CREED:

NOTES:

NOTES:

NOTES:

NOTES: